9 ESSENTIAL SKILLS TO

MASTER

BOYS AGED 8-14

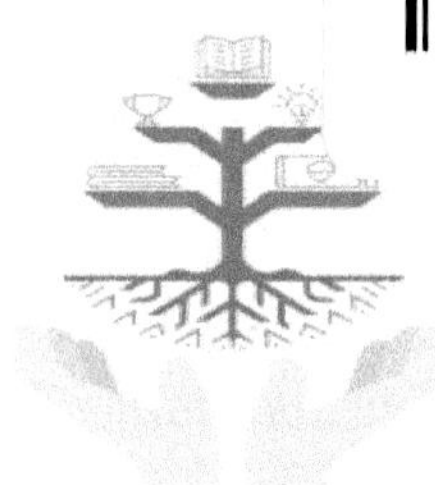

Fun Skills
A guide to growing up strong, smart and capable

FABIAN CHOW

First edition

This book has been professionally typeset for publication using Microsoft Word.

AUTHOR'S BIO

FABIAN CHOW

They say life begins at 40, but I say it begins whenever you decide to live it king-size! Well, here I am - a veteran who traded in his dog tags for a pen (and maybe a spatula, because who doesn't love a good soufflé?). As a veteran, author, gourmand, and globe-trotter - I believe in chasing dreams until the last note plays. From the battlefield to the bookshelf, my journey has been filled with unexpected twists and turns, delicious food, and unforgettable adventures. I'm living proof that it's never too late to chase your dreams, even if those dreams involve questionable culinary experiments and a passport full of stamps.

When not conquering the world one delicious dish at a time or lost in a foreign land, I'm usually found nose-deep in a good book or lost in a symphony of sound. My motto? Keep smiling, keep cooking, keep exploring, and always, always chase those dreams (before they chase you!).

I believe in the power of dreams and the importance of leaving a legacy, one delicious recipe and one exciting adventure at a time. I hope my books bring you as much joy as writing them.

So, grab a copy, buckle up, and get ready for a wild ride!

PREFACE

Hey there - If you've picked up this book, then I know one thing about you already—you're someone who's curious, brave, and ready to discover what it takes to be awesome! Whether you're 8, 10, or 14, this book was written with you in mind because this is your time to shine. Life between 8 and 14 can feel like an adventure, sometimes exciting and fun, and other times confusing and challenging. But guess what? Every hero needs skills to conquer their journey. That's what this book is all about helping you master nine powerful skills that will make you stronger, kinder, and smarter—not just for today, but for the rest of your life. You'll learn how to stay positive when things get tough, how to be resilient like a superhero who gets back up after a fall, and how to make changes that turn challenges into opportunities. Ready for an adventure? Let's be honest: growing up can be tricky. There's a lot to figure out, from navigating friendships and dealing with schoolwork to understanding your emotions and setting goals. What if there were secret skills that could help you succeed at school, ace friendships, and navigate all the challenges life throws your way? Well, then, this isn't your typical dusty old textbook. This is a mission briefing, a survival guide, a cheat code for life! Inside, you'll discover nine essential skills that are way more exciting than any video game. We're talking about levelling up your life—building confidence, making awesome friends, and mastering challenges that will pop up along the way. This book is your secret weapon—a guide packed with practical skills to help you navigate the ups and downs of being a boy aged 8-14. Inside, you'll uncover nine essential skills—powerful tools that will unlock your potential and help you become the best version of yourself. Forget boring lectures; this is a hands-on guide with cool tips, awesome tricks, and real-world scenarios that will help you conquer anything that comes your way. Get ready to level up your life! buckle up, grab your gear, and let's get started!

- *Fabian Chow*

FOREWORD

Young men,

I've spent a lifetime navigating complex challenges, from the battlefields of Kargil, Kashmir and Africa to the halls of the South Block in New Delhi. Through it all, I've learned that success isn't just about talent or good luck; it's about mastering essential skills – the building blocks upon which you construct a life of purpose and accomplishment.

This book by Fabian, offers you nine such building blocks, carefully selected to help you thrive in the years ahead. These aren't just abstract concepts; they're practical tools that you can apply immediately. They're the foundation upon which you will build confidence, forge strong relationships, and navigate the many opportunities and challenges that await you.

Throughout my career, I've emphasized the importance of preparation and planning. This book provides precisely that – a plan to equip yourselves with skills vital for success in school, in your personal lives, and ultimately, in the world. Mastering these skills will not only help you succeed but will also empower you to make a positive difference in the lives of others.

Remember, leadership isn't just about being in charge; it's about knowing how to work effectively with others, communicating clearly, and achieving common goals. The skills outlined in this book will help you become strong leaders, not just for yourselves but also for your communities.

I urge you to approach this book not as a chore but as an opportunity. Embrace the lessons within, practice the skills diligently, and watch as you build a future based on competence, resilience, and purpose.

With great confidence in your potential,

- General Rajinder Dewan, AVSM, VSM
  Indian Armed Forces

BOOK DESCRIPTION

Welcome to TEENHOOD—the most exciting yet challenging time of your life! The tween years are an important time to learn and discover the world and shape who you will be in it. While these are exciting times, they can also be tricky. Pre-teens means dealing with big emotions and physical changes that they may not feel equipped to handle. Learn **Comprehensive Life Skills:** Master essential skills for academic, emotional, and social success. They may feel unsure of how to behave or what to do in certain situations. They may be worried about making friends or dealing with increased responsibilities and stress. The great news is that they're not alone. **Ready to unlock your teen superpowers?** Picture yourself thriving—not just surviving—through academic pressures, emotional well-being, healthy relationships, social challenges, and real-world responsibilities.

Are these challenges familiar to you?

- Overwhelmed by the constant pressure of school and the struggle to find balance?
- Finding it hard to make the right decisions when faced with peer pressure?

- Curious about effective communication with family and friends?
- Feeling trapped by anxiety or lost in feelings of isolation?
- Looking for ways to boost your self-confidence and embrace your uniqueness?
- Need money management skills to manage your finances effectively?
- Feeling the weight of handling stuff on your own and wondering how you can multiply your efforts to do many things at once?
- Searching for practical tips on basic domestic skills and wondering if you will ever be independent?

If you answered **'yes'** to any of these, **your roadmap to turning these challenges into opportunities begins here!** Embark on a transformative journey with "*9 Essential Skills to Master for Boys 8-14*". This book is your go-to guide through the whirlwind of teen-hood, offering practical solutions to tackle the biggest challenges you face. It's designed to empower you to navigate this crucial phase with confidence and independence.

Inside, you'll discover:

- How to embrace Change and live a life of Positivity and Gratitude.

- Healthy Habits & Self-Care: Essential practices, bonus tips, and recipes for a balanced and fulfilling life.
- Cook a delicious meal, take care of your environment and deal with emergencies.
- Building Relationships: Strengthen communication skills for lasting connections and making friends.
- work as part of a TEAM and build lasting relationships.
- Emotional Well-Being: Mindful exercises to reduce stress deal with strong emotions and become resilient.
- Develop a strong, dependable and confident personality.
- Communicate clearly and effectively.
- Digital Literacy: Navigate the digital world safely and responsibly in today's tech-driven era. Stay safe online
- Financial Literacy: Understand money, budget & handle money responsibly. Learn budgeting and money management for long-term success.
- Set SMART goals to achieve your dreams.

Perfect for teens, parents, and educators looking to empower the next generation. But that's not all! **There's so much more to explore.** It features fun activities and interactive tools that make learning and self-discovery exciting. Every exercise is crafted to help you build unshakable confidence and develop the life skills you need to thrive as you grow into a capable, resilient young adult. **Let's dive in and uncover a world full of solutions to your teenage challenges.**

Don't wait—your journey to confidence and success begins today!

Grab your copy now and start thriving!

Table of Contents

Habits are powerful, whether you realize it or not. They shape everything you do; from the time you wake up to when you go to sleep. Just like physical exercise helps your body grow stronger, practicing good habits helps your character grow.

Think of your growth as a building, and each habit you form is a brick. Every day, you lay another brick in the structure of who you're becoming.

Now ask yourself—what kind of bricks are you using? Are you building something solid or just throwing things together that won't hold up over time?

INTRODUCTION

To the finder of this book:

Congratulations! You have just stumbled upon a secret manual containing wisdom that has guided boys to become the best versions of themselves. Use it wisely, and your life will never be the same.

I recall being your age like it was yesterday. I was a carefree kid one minute, and the next, bam! - my teenage years hit me like a curveball. I wasn't prepared for the challenges that came with the teenage years, yet they awaited me like hungry wolves at the edge of a cliff, ready to pounce at any moment. But I felt invincible in figuring out who I was as I walked through that situation with school and friends.

Now, I know what you're thinking. "That was ages ago! Things are different now." And you're right. We didn't have smartphones or social media when I was your age. But even without all the accessible tech, Life was still complicated. I had to figure out how to fit in, stand up for myself, and make wise choices. I still remember wishing I had some manual to help me.

Now that I'm grown up with kids, I've had the opportunity to watch them go through their own adventures. Sure, their challenges might have looked different, but the root of what they faced is similar to what I dealt with in the past. It's still about feeling unsure, coping with peer pressure, and trying to understand who you truly are.

I'll be real for a second. Life today moves super-fast. There's a lot of pressure to keep up with everything happening online, at school, and with friends. I get it—it's more challenging now. But the good news is you've got access to a wealth of information and resources that we could only dream of back in the day. This book is just one example of that.

Over the years, I've discovered something unique. It wasn't a physical object I could hold in my hands. No, it was a set of skills and mindsets that changed everything. At first, I didn't believe it. I mean, how can something so simple make such a big difference? But it did, and I wish I had known about it when I was younger. Even though the world may have changed, the skills you need to handle it haven't, and I'm excited to share them with you.

Before we get started, I've got a few questions for you:

- Have you ever had those days where everything feels like a challenge? Let's say you're in gym class, trying to win a game, but nothing is going your way. Or you're in class, figuring out a math problem that won't make sense. Or you're sitting alone at the cafeteria at lunch, wishing you knew how to start a conversation with someone.

- Or do you sometimes feel like the world is just too complicated? Like a lot is going on, and you're expected to handle it all but you're not quite sure how?

Trust me, you're not alone. Even us adults still struggle sometimes. But there are ways to make it all easier. That's exactly what we're going to explore together. But first, let me tell you about a kid named Sam.

Sam used to worry about everything. Getting called by the teacher in class? Terrifying. Need to remember to bring his homework? Major disaster. Tripping in the middle of the cafeteria with his tray in his hand? The end of the world.

But then, something changed for Sam. He learned a simple skill that helped him stay calm even when things went wrong. It didn't mean life became perfect for him—he still had hard days, but he learned how to handle them this time. He didn't let minor problems turn into big ones anymore. He discovered the ability to bounce back, no matter what. This is what I call resilience.

Now, Sam didn't learn resilience and become a superhero for himself overnight. He, too, had to find something to guide him, the same way you have found this book. I'm telling you, you have the skills, just like Sam discovered, that can help you face anything life throws your way. I'm talking about skills like:

- Staying positive, even when things aren't going right.
- Thinking fast so you can solve problems quickly, whether during a tough test or an argument with a friend.

- Being someone everyone can count on.
- Handling change, so when things don't go as planned, you can remain calm and figure out your next play.

You may not have unlocked it yet, but these skills are already inside you, waiting to be unlocked. All you need is the right key. And guess what? This book is that key.

These skills are like tools in a toolbox. I'm sure you know carpenters do not only use a hammer for every piece of furniture they work on. Well, these skills work the same way. Sometimes, you need teamwork to get through a challenging project at school. Other times, it's about staying positive when things aren't going your way because the more tools you have, the better prepared you'll be for whatever comes your way. I didn't always have the right tools when I was younger. I had to learn the hard way. But you? You've got a head start.

"I'd rather be playing video games?"

"What if this book doesn't even help me at all?"

These are questions that might be nagging you in the back of your mind. It's normal to have these doubts. But don't let them stop you. Think of this book as your first mission. If you can make it through this, it shows you've got the courage and discipline to face new challenges head-on.

I completely understand that trying new things can be scary. It's like your mom telling you you're about to start at a new school or your dad telling you to try out for a sports team. It feels like a big deal. You're nervous. What if you mess up? What if people laugh? What if you're just... not good enough?

Now, think about how different you would feel knowing exactly what to do at that moment. This can only happen when you learn to embrace challenge and change. You begin to feel more powerful when you stop worrying about the "what ifs" and focus on what you can do. The funny thing about fear? Once you face it, it gets smaller. And when you face it with the right skills, it disappears.

Also, think about your favorite video game. Each level has new challenges, right? Sometimes, you must think fast; other times, you must work with your team. As you play, you learn. You get better. With time, you start to figure out the tricks that make the next level easier. Life is the same way. Each day is a new level, with new challenges. The more skills you have, the more you level up. This book works the same way. It will help you find the tricks and skills to master every level life throws at you.

Now, don't get me wrong. I'm not here to tell you how to live your life. But I am here to share what I've learned—from my own experiences and watching my kids face their own challenges. What we are going to deal with together is this:

- How to stay cool when things get stressful.
- How to be a good friend and teammate.
- How to turn problems into opportunities.
- How to keep going, even when it feels hard.

Your mission throughout this book, should you choose to accept it, is to unlock the secrets to becoming awesome at life. All you need to do is jump in, try out the challenges, and see what happens. The more you practice, the better you'll get!

So, if you're ready, let's get started! By the end of this book, I promise you'll be a brand-new version of yourself—smarter, stronger, and ready for anything.

"A problem is a chance for you to do your best"

- Duke Ellington.

SKILL: 1 THE POWER TRIO: GRATITUDE, POSITIVITY, CHANGE

Life is a wild adventure, full of ups and downs, challenges and triumphs. Think about a puzzle. When you first open the box, all you see are scattered pieces, and it's hard to figure out how they'll fit together. At first glance, they might look random and disconnected. But you know, deep down, that when you start putting those pieces in the right places, they'll reveal a complete picture.

To navigate this journey with strength and resilience, it is essential to cultivate a powerful trio of skills: Gratitude, Positivity, and Change. Each one is like a puzzle piece. On their own, they're useful, but they don't show the whole picture. Practicing just gratitude is excellent, but without positivity, it's hard to see how you can grow from the tough times. And without embracing change, it's hard to stay open to new possibilities. When woven together, something powerful happens. These three create an inner compass as the pieces connect, guiding you through life's twists and turns, helping you overcome obstacles and embrace opportunities with a sense of purpose and joy.

Imagine a world where you focus on the good things, even in difficult times, and actively search for the positive aspects of every experience, big or small. This is the power of gratitude—appreciating what you have, even when things aren't perfect.

But what happens when things don't go your way? That's where positivity comes in. This is about seeing the good in every situation, even when it's hard. It's about keeping a hopeful outlook and believing in your ability to overcome challenges.

And finally, change. Life constantly evolves, and embracing change is crucial to growth and success. It's about accepting that things will shift, learning to adapt, and finding the courage to step out of your comfort zone.

Together, these three skills form a robust foundation for a fulfilling life. They empower you to face adversity with strength, find joy every day, and embrace the exciting journey ahead. This is the essence of skill number 1—it's not about focusing on just one thing. It's about understanding how these habits work together to create a better version of you.

This brings us to the first of our trio: Gratitude.

Gratitude

One morning, a blind boy sat on the steps of a busy building, holding a sign that said, "I'm blind; please help." He had a small hat at his feet, but there were only a few coins inside—just spare change from the people who rushed by without really stopping to notice him.

After a while, a man passed by. He paused, dropped a few coins into the boy's hat, and then picked up the sign. He turned it around, scribbled something new, and placed it back in the boy's hands so everyone walking by could see the new message.

As the day went on, something amazing happened—more and more people stopped to give money to the boy. His hat, which had been almost empty that morning, started to fill up quickly.

Later that afternoon, the man returned to see how things were going. Hearing the man's footsteps, the boy asked, "Are you the one who changed my sign? What did you write?"

The man smiled and replied, "I just wrote the same truth differently. Your sign said you were blind, but I added something for people to think about."

He had written, "Today is a beautiful day, but I can't see it."

Both signs told the truth, but the new one made people stop and realize how lucky they were to enjoy the simple things—like being able to see. It reminded them to be grateful for what they had.

Here's a thought for you.

What's the first thing you do when you wake up in the morning? Do you hit the snooze button? Check your phone? Or maybe you jump right into the day without thinking. Have you ever thought about what might happen if you took a moment to be thankful instead of rushing into things?

I'm not talking about sitting down for a prayer or anything like that. I mean something as simple as thinking, "I'm glad I finished my homework last night," or "I'm lucky to have friends to hang out with at school today." Just a quick moment to recognize the good stuff.

Gratitude isn't just about saying "thank you" when someone holds the door open for you or when you get a present. It is about noticing the good things in your life and taking a moment to appreciate them.

When you practice gratitude, you shift your focus away from what you don't have to what you do. And trust me, that small shift can change everything.

You might be thinking, "Why should I care about this gratitude stuff?" Well, let me ask you this: Have you ever had one of those days when everything seems wrong? Maybe you overslept, got a bad grade on a test, or had a fight with a friend. It's easy to get stuck feeling like the whole world is against you, right? But what if, in the middle of that bad day, you paused for just a second and thought, "Even though I messed up today, I know my parents still love me. Yes, they may get mad, but they still love me, and I'd still eat dinner."

That's what gratitude does—it helps you see the good in the bad, the light in the dark. It doesn't mean pretending that everything's perfect, but it enables you to realize that even on tough days, there's something to be thankful for. Suddenly, things that seemed annoying, dull, or even upsetting start looking slightly different.

Why is this habit so important anyway?

Well, gratitude is like a superpower for your brain. Research shows that people who regularly practice gratitude are happier, less stressed, and even sleep better. When you focus on the good stuff, your brain starts to notice more of it. It's like flipping a switch that makes you see things differently.

Take school, for example. Maybe you've got a class that you're not a big fan of. The teacher gives too much homework, and you don't really like the subject. But what if you looked for something in that class to be thankful for? Maybe there's a classmate who makes you laugh, or you enjoy the moments when the teacher gives you a break to chat with your friends. When you focus on those things, the class doesn't seem so bad anymore, does it?

As your face starts scrunching up in annoyance when the time for the class draws near, the moment you realize that one thing that doesn't make the class all that bad, you suddenly find your lips quirking up to form a smile. Without you even knowing it!

Also, gratitude isn't just for things—it's for people, too. Think about your friendships. How do you feel when someone appreciates you for something you've done? It feels good, right? Your relationships get stronger when you show appreciation to your friends, family, or even your teachers. They see that you value them, and that brings you closer.

So, how do you actually practice gratitude?

It's easier than you think. Here are some simple ways to get started:

Gratitude Journaling

Before you roll your eyes, hear me out! Writing down three things you're grateful for every day can really make a difference. They don't have to be big things. It could be something as small as "I'm grateful the rain didn't fall today and I was able to play football" or "I'm thankful I had my favorite snack at lunch."

At the end of the day, before bed, revisit your journal and read everything you've written for the day. As you do, notice how your smile gets bigger and how excited you become for the next day. This act of writing and revisiting helps to lock it into your brain. And locking it in your brain means that over time, your mind will naturally start to focus on the positives without even trying.

It's like training a muscle—the more you work at it, the stronger it becomes. Soon enough, you'll find that gratitude is no longer something you have to remind yourself to practice; it will simply be a part of who you are.

Gratitude Check-Ins

If you don't want to go the route of journaling, there's an easier option. Pick a time of day to do a quick check-in with yourself. Maybe it's when you wake up or right before you go to bed (remember to set an alarm for this so you don't forget). Take 60 seconds (or more, depending on how much time you can spare) to think of one thing that went well that day or something you're thankful for.

It's a simple habit, but it sets the tone for your day or helps you sleep with a positive mindset. But notice that as you start thinking about the good stuff, the not-so-good moments come up, too. That's one difference between journaling and this method. When you journal, your mind is focused only on the good things you've written down, so it's easier to center your thoughts on positivity. But when you're reflecting mentally, you have to scan through your whole day, and sometimes, the bad stuff pops up along the way.

Here's the key: don't dwell on those tough moments. That's not your goal. Instead, focus on finding the good in those challenges. Ask yourself, "How did I get through that situation?" Think about what helped you cope, and be grateful for your resilience or the people who supported you. By doing this, you're training yourself to see the silver lining, even in difficult times. And that's where real growth begins.

Expressing Gratitude to Others

Gratitude isn't just something you do in solitude or keep to yourself. It's not just about saying "I'm thankful" in your mind. Gratitude also extends to the people who make the good things in your life happen. When someone helps you out, says something kind, or even makes you laugh, don't keep that feeling to yourself—share it. Saying something as simple as "Thanks for that" goes a long way in making both you and the other person feel good.

But gratitude isn't only for the good things—it works even in tough moments. Remember the example of "Even though my grades aren't great, I know my parents still love me, and I'll still get dinner"? Let's dig deeper into that. Imagine you've gotten a bad grade. When you get home, even before showing your parents the grades, say something like, "Mom, Dad, I'm really grateful for how much you love me and how much effort you put into my education. I don't take it for granted, and I promise to do great even though I didn't do well this time. I hope my dinners still guaranteed tonight."

Now, do this and see how the situation might shift. Sure, your parents might still be upset (a bad grade is a bad grade), but starting with gratitude can soften the blow. By showing appreciation and responsibility, you're not only reminding them of your effort but also helping turn what could be a tense moment into something constructive. And trust me, the reaction you get will likely be much more understanding than if you went in without expressing gratitude.

The Gratitude Reset

When you're in the middle of a stressful or annoying situation, it's easy to focus only on what's going wrong. But here's a challenge: stop for a moment and find one thing to be grateful for, even if it feels hard. Let's say you're struggling with a challenging math problem in class. Instead of getting frustrated, you could think, "I'm grateful I have a teacher who's willing to help if I ask," or

"I'm thankful I have friends who can explain this after class."

Or imagine you've had an argument with a friend. You could stop and think, "I'm grateful we've been friends long enough to know we can work through this," or "I'm thankful I have other friends I can talk to while we cool off."

The key is to shift your focus from what's going wrong to what's still well, even in that moment. The more you practice finding those little things, the easier it gets to deal with the stress. Over time, you'll start to notice that even in the middle of chaos, there's always something to appreciate.

Challenge For You

Practice gratitude for the next week. Write down three things each day for which you're thankful. By the end of the week, notice how much more positive you feel.

Positivity

Now, positivity often gets misunderstood. Some people think being positive means ignoring the bad stuff and pretending everything's fine. But that's not it at all. Positivity is about how you choose to respond when things *aren't* perfect. It's not about ignoring problems but facing them with the mindset that you can handle whatever comes next.

Think about this—have you ever noticed how some people seem to bounce back quickly from tough situations while others stay stuck, feeling defeated? The difference often lies in their mindset. People who cultivate positivity aren't immune to bad days or struggles; they just choose to focus on solutions instead of staying stuck on the problem.

Let's look at an example: Imagine you've studied hard for a test, but when the results come back, you didn't do as well as you hoped. You could let that disappointment ruin your mood, or you could take a different approach. Sure, it's okay to feel frustrated—that's normal. But instead of staying there, you could remind yourself, "I'll study harder next time" or "I've learned what I need to work on." This shift in thinking doesn't erase the problem, but it helps you move forward with a clearer, more positive mindset.

Positivity also affects the people around you. Ever notice how spending time with someone who's always complaining can bring your mood down? On the flip side, being around someone who sees the brighter side of things can make you feel better, even when things aren't perfect. That's the power of positivity—it's contagious.

Here's the good news: cultivating positivity isn't something you're born with or without. It's a skill you can practice, just like anything else. And the more you practice, the better you get. So, how do you do it? Here are a few ways to start:

Reframing Negative Thoughts

Negative thoughts have a way of creeping up on you—sometimes without you even realizing it. It's normal—we all experience them, and sometimes we can't help it. But what you can do is reframe them. When something goes wrong, don't jump to "This is awful." Instead, use your gratitude habit to shift your thinking. Ask yourself, "What's one good thing that came from this?" or "What can I learn from this?" For example, if you didn't do well on a test, instead of thinking, “I’m terrible at this,” you could reframe it to “Now I know what I need to work on.”

Surrounding Yourself with Positive Influences

The people and environments you spend time in significantly impact your mindset. Remember how we talked about positivity being contagious? When you choose to hang out with friends who lift you up, their positive energy rubs off on you, making it easier to stay positive. On the other hand, spending too much time around people who constantly complain or focus on the negatives can bring your mood down and make it harder to stay upbeat.

That’s why it’s essential to create spaces—both online and offline—that encourage positive thinking. Surround yourself with people, places, and activities that make you feel good and support your growth. When you do that, you’ll notice how much easier it is to keep a positive mindset, even when things get tough.

Using Positive Affirmations

I know what you're about to say and do—roll your eyes and think, "Affirmations? Really?" But let me convince you otherwise. Affirmations work. That's why the hype around them never fades. Remember what we said about the brain earlier—how it starts to adapt when you keep doing something repeatedly? Well, when you take that extra effort to repeat positive affirmations daily, you're training your brain to believe in those positive statements. Over time, these affirmations help you develop a more confident, resilient mindset.

You can start with these simple affirmations—repeat them to yourself daily, and watch how they help you build confidence and stay positive:

- I am capable of handling anything that comes my way.
- I am grateful for today and all its opportunities.
- I believe in my abilities and will do my best.
- I choose kindness and respect for everyone.

- I welcome challenges because it helps me grow.
- I am surrounded by love, and I trust my journey.
- I am growing stronger and smarter every day.
- I am proud of my progress, even the small steps.
- I can face challenges with a positive attitude.
- I learn from my mistakes and keep moving forward.
- I have the power to turn tough situations into learning opportunities.
- I am worthy of success and happiness.
- I embrace change as a chance to grow and improve.

And if you still feel embarrassed to start, there's no need to make a big show of it. You can do it secretly—just mutter the affirmations to yourself, say them in your mind, or even head to the restroom for a quick pep talk in the mirror. The point is the more you do it, the easier it gets, and soon, you'll notice the shift in how you handle tough situations.

Celebrating Small Wins

You don't have to wait for big achievements to feel good about yourself. Celebrate the small victories, too, like finishing an assignment early or handling a tough conversation with a friend. And here's where the first habit we talked about—gratitude—comes into play. The more you notice and are grateful for those small successes, the more positivity you'll naturally bring into your daily life. It's all connected—gratitude fuels positivity, and positivity helps you stay focused on growth, even in the smallest of victories.

Change

If there's one thing you can count on in life, it's that things are constantly changing. Whether it's starting a new school year, dealing with shifting friendships, or adjusting to a new routine, change is a part of life. But here's the catch: while change can be scary, it can also be an opportunity for growth.

Think about it. When something unexpected happens—maybe it was switching schools, making new friends, or dealing with a family move—your first reaction might be frustration or fear. But after some time, you'd likely adjust to the new normal and maybe even find some good in it. That's what embracing change is all about—it's like practicing gratitude and positivity but applied to new situations. You train your brain to think, "What can I be grateful for in this change?" or "How can I use this new situation to grow?"

So, how do you start embracing change instead of fighting it? Let's break it down:

Step 1: Keep an Open Mind

When something changes, instead of immediately thinking, "This is going to be terrible," pause for a moment and try to keep an open mind. Ask yourself, "What could be good about this? What could I learn from this experience?"

One secret that life doesn't want you to know is that change often brings new opportunities, even if it doesn't seem that way initially.

Step 2: Focus on What You Can Control

Change can make you feel like you've lost control, but the truth is, you always have control over *something*. Maybe you can't control switching schools, but you can control how you approach making new friends. Focus on the things you can influence, and you'll feel more confident and less stressed.

Step 3: Learn to Adapt

Think of yourself like a tree. When the wind blows hard, a tree bends but doesn't break. You can learn to bend with the changes in your life, too. Doing this means finding ways to adjust and keep moving forward. The more flexible you are, the easier it is to handle whatever comes your way.

Step 4: Turn Change into an Opportunity

Sometimes, change feels like a door slamming shut. But if you look closely, another door may be opening. For example, if a close friend moves away, it might feel like the end of the world. But what if that opens up space for you to get to know someone else better or to strengthen your connection with friends you already have? Finding the opportunity in change takes practice, but the more you do it, the more you'll start to see new possibilities.

Let me tell you about Alex, a 12-year-old kid who had a pretty rough year. His grades were slipping, he wasn't getting along with his friends like he used to, and on top of it all, his parents were going through a divorce. It felt like everything was going out of control, and no matter what he did, things just didn't seem to improve.

Alex didn't know how to deal with it all. He was frustrated and angry, and honestly, he felt stuck. His teacher noticed this, and one day, she pulled him aside and sent him to the guidance counselor's office. Alex didn't want to be there. He figured the counsellor would give him some advice that would just go in one ear and out the other. But he had no choice, so he sat there and listened.

The counsellor talked to Alex about focusing on three things: **Gratitude**, **Positivity**, and **Embracing Change**. Alex wasn't convinced. It all sounded nice, but what difference would it really make? However, as he left the office that day, he had a thought. Maybe if he started doing something good, the universe might start listening to him. If he started thanking the universe instead of blaming it, maybe things would turn around. And, in the back of his mind, he hoped that if he got good grades and became a "good kid," his parents might notice and stay together.

His reasons for getting started may sound silly, but at least they were enough to push him into action. So, Alex decided to give **gratitude** a try first. He started small, noticing little things he could be thankful for each day—his favorite lunch, a sunny day, or when his teacher didn't assign too much homework. At first, it was part of his plan to get the universe on his side, but as he kept going, something unexpected happened. Practicing gratitude actually made him feel better, even if the big problems in his life weren't changing right away.

Next, he worked on **positivity**. This was even harder for Alex, especially with everything going on. But instead of focusing on how bad things were, he started asking himself, "What can I do better?" or "What's one thing I can improve?" A test was coming up soon, and he needed to prove himself, even if it was just in half his courses. So he started pushing himself, finding ways to study that worked better for him. He even began asking his teachers for extra help.

Alex didn't perform as well as he had hoped when the test results came in. He did well in two courses but not as well in the others. However, instead of feeling defeated and giving up, Alex's attitude toward **gratitude and positivity** made him see things differently. A few months ago, he had been failing all his courses, and now he had excelled in two and done decently in the rest. Change doesn't happen overnight—it takes time. Alex chose to be grateful for his progress and used that as motivation to keep working harder for the next opportunity.

That's when Alex began to understand the importance of **embracing change**. Even though Alex hated that his family life was different now, he realized that fighting the changes wasn't making things easier—it was making them harder. Alex still wished his parents would stay together, but he slowly realized that some things were beyond his control. What he could control, though, was how he responded to the changes. So, Alex found ways to stay connected with his parents, even though they weren't together anymore. And he realized that adapting to these changes didn't mean losing everything good in his life—it just meant things were going to be a little different.

As Alex practiced these three skills—gratitude, positivity, and embracing change—he realized something important. At first, he thought doing all of this would fix his problems, like some magic solution. However, as Alex continued, he started to see that his reasons for getting started were less important than what he gained from the process. The more Alex practiced these habits, the happier and more confident he became, regardless of the outcome.

PRACTICAL EXERCISE 1

1. Think about a recent change in your life. What was the change?

____

____

____

____

____

____

2. How did you feel when this change happened?

____

____

____

____

____

____

3. Did you find it difficult to accept the change at first? What made it hard, or what helped you adjust?

____

____

____

____

____

____

4. Was there anything positive that came out of it? Maybe you learned something new or met new people.

____

____

____

____

____

____

5. When you found something good to focus on, how did it make you feel? Did it help you handle the change better or see things differently?

____

____

____

____

____

____

6. Now, think about someone or something that helped you during this change. How can you show your appreciation for that?

____

____

____

____

“Why fit in when you were born to ‘Stand Out’

- *Dr Seuss*

SKILL 2: BASIC DOMESTIC SKILLS

Have you ever had that moment when your mom or dad asked you to help out with chores, and you sighed, thinking, "Why do I have to do this?" I get it. You'd rather spend your time doing something fun or relaxing. But here's the thing: your teen years are the perfect time to learn these essential skills. It might sound stressful, and let's be honest—nobody loves doing chores. But nobody is going to take the time to teach a grown adult how to do these basic things they should have learned years ago.

You might be thinking, "But I'm a boy; isn't this different for me?" Well, that's where you're mistaken. It's 2024! Everyone—no matter their gender—needs to know how to take care of themselves. Learning these skills is not just about helping out at home; it's about gaining independence, confidence, and the ability to handle life on your terms.

So, it's about time you stopped sighing about chores and started feeling like a pro in your own home. Let's get you equipped, starting with cleaning!

Cleaning

"Boys are messy."

I'm sure you've heard this many times. It's like there's this idea going around that if you're a boy, your room probably looks like a tornado hit it. But is that really true for you? Or are you the exception who proves that idea wrong? Well, even if you are not, today is the day you are reborn to become the tidiest human on Earth!

Think about it. How does it feel to leave your room untidy? I know you're probably used to seeing your space in disarray, and it doesn't really bother you anymore. But take a glance at your room right now and think about how you feel about it. It kind of messes with your head, right? Deep down, you wish you could just pack those clothes off the chair, pick up that wrapper from the floor, and restore some order. Yes? No?

No?

Okay. Think about when you lost your favorite game controller in a sea of dirty clothes. Or you couldn't find your homework because your desk was buried under a mountain of stuff. Now, that was frustrating, right?

Let's be real for a second: the mess doesn't just happen overnight. It's a result of small, repetitive actions—like tossing clothes on the floor instead of putting them away—that gradually lead to chaos.

Here's a scenario: you're in a rush to get to school, and you need to find the perfect outfit. You dig through your closet, pulling out clothes and tossing aside those that don't cut. After a long day at school, you come home tired, and instead of putting your clothes back in the closet, you drop them on the floor, thinking, "I'll take care of this later."

Repeat this process a few times throughout the week, and suddenly, you're standing in a sea of clothes, shoes, and items that have found their way to the floor. It's overwhelming! Now, instead of having a nice, organized space to chill out in, you're faced with a messy room that makes you feel stressed and distracted.

When I say "clean," I don't mean you have to scrub every inch of your room until it sparkles (though that wouldn't be a bad thing!). What I'm talking about is tidying up. Now, I know what you're thinking: "Tidying up? Boring!" But trust me, it's actually one of the most valuable skills you'll ever learn. It's so important that there's even a famous saying about it: "Cleanliness is next to godliness."

A clean room isn't just aesthetically pleasing; it also significantly impacts your mental and emotional well-being. When your space is tidy, it's easier to focus. You feel more relaxed and less anxious, which is essential for your overall happiness. On the flip side, living in a cluttered environment can lead to overwhelming and stressful feelings. You might find it hard to concentrate when your mind is distracted by the mess around you.

A clean room can serve as a sanctuary where you can unwind, recharge, and get creative. Think about it: it feels easier to think clearly and make decisions when everything is in its place. Plus, keeping your space clean shows you respect yourself and your belongings. It's a way of saying, "I value my space, and I care about how I feel in it." Even when you have friends over, you'll feel proud to show them your room rather than feeling embarrassed by the mess.

So, how do you break this cycle of messiness and create a clean, welcoming space? It all starts with understanding that keeping your room tidy requires a commitment to small, consistent habits. Cleaning isn't just about one big effort; it's about maintaining order daily.

Now, let's get into some practical tricks that can help you maintain a tidy space without it feeling like a chore.

Set a Daily Cleaning Routine

Establishing a cleaning routine is one of the best ways to keep your room tidy. This doesn't mean you have to spend hours cleaning every day; even just 5-10 minutes can make a big difference. For example, set a timer each evening for 10 minutes and focus on picking up any clothes on the floor, straightening your desk, or wiping down surfaces.

Use Storage Solutions

Invest in some storage bins or boxes to help keep your things organized. You can use these to sort items like toys, books, or sports gear. Label the boxes so you know where everything belongs. This way, when it's time to clean, you can quickly toss things into their designated spots.

Make Cleaning a Family Affair

If your family members are around, involve them in the cleaning process. Create a "clean-up challenge" where everyone competes to see who can tidy their space the fastest. Not only does this make cleaning more fun, but it also fosters teamwork and responsibility within your household.

The 5-Minute Rule

When you notice something out of place, take five minutes to put it back where it belongs. Whether it's a stray book, a piece of clothing, or even a dirty dish, taking a few moments to tidy up can prevent messes from accumulating.

Be Mindful of Your Space

When you're done with something, whether it is a snack or a gaming session, make it a habit to clean up after yourself immediately. This could mean throwing away wrappers, putting dishes in the sink, or storing your game controllers in their designated spots. The more you practice this habit, the less clutter will build up.

Create a Cleaning Playlist

Turn cleaning into a fun activity by creating a playlist of your favorite songs. Play your tunes while you tidy up, and you'll find that cleaning becomes a lot more enjoyable. You'll be surprised at how much you can accomplish when you're having fun!

Cleaning may seem like a chore, but with the right mindset and habits, it can become a simple part of your routine—a way to show love and respect for your space. Remember, a tidy room is more than just a pretty sight; it's a foundation for a happier, healthier you.

Laundry

Laundry? Isn't that just more cleaning?

Well, yes and no. While cleaning focuses on tidying up your space, laundry is about taking care of your clothes and ensuring they're fresh, clean, and ready to wear. Think of laundry as an extension of the cleaning habits we discussed earlier. Just as a messy room doesn't clean itself, that pile of laundry won't vanish on its own.

But laundry is not just about tossing clothes into the washing machine and hitting "start." It’s a multi-step process that begins with sorting out what to wash and ends with neatly folding and putting everything away in your wardrobe. Each step is crucial to ensure that your clothes stay in excellent condition and that your laundry experience is efficient and effective.

But laundry is not just about tossing clothes into the washing machine and hitting "start." It's a multi-step process that begins with sorting out what to wash and ends with neatly folding and putting everything away in your wardrobe. Each step is important to ensure that your clothes stay in excellent condition.

Here's something you might not have thought about: clean clothes are like your personal billboard! They tell others a lot about who you are before you even say a word. Imagine meeting your crush or a new friend while wearing dirty shirt or clothes that smell like yesterday's gym class – not the best first impression, right?

Think about it – when you're wearing clean, neat clothes, people are more likely to want to hang out with you, sit next to you in class, or pick you for their team. Nobody wants to be around someone with funky-smelling clothes! Plus, girls especially notice these things (trust me on this one). They tend to appreciate guys who take care of themselves and their appearance.

Bad odors from sweaty or unwashed clothes are like invisible force fields that push people away. But, clean, fresh-smelling clothes help others see you in the best light possible and make you feel confident.

The Laundry Process: Step by Step

The steps below will teach you how to do your laundry like a pro!

Step 1: Sorting

Like cleaning your room, the first step in doing laundry is sorting your clothes. Create separate piles for darks, lights, and whites. This prevents colors from bleeding onto each other. For instance, you wouldn't want your favorite white t-shirt to turn pink because you tossed it in with a red hoodie.

Here's a pro tip to save your clothes from color disasters: Before you throw new colored clothes into the washing machine, try this simple test. Take your new item (like that awesome new red gaming t-shirt or those cool blue jeans) and test it for colorfastness (a fancy way of saying "checking if the color will run).

Here's how to do it:

- Find a hidden spot on your new clothes (like an inside seam)
- Wet a white cotton swab or small white cloth
- Gently rub it on that hidden spot
- If you see color transfer to the white cloth or swab, your item is likely to bleed!

Think of sorting laundry like organizing your gaming cards or LEGO sets - keeping similar things together is always the smart move.

Step 2: Check the Labels

Before throwing anything into the washing machine, take a second to check the care labels on your clothes. These labels tell you how to wash and dry each item. Some clothes can handle hot water, while others need to be washed in cold. Ignore these instructions, and you're heading towards a washing disaster.

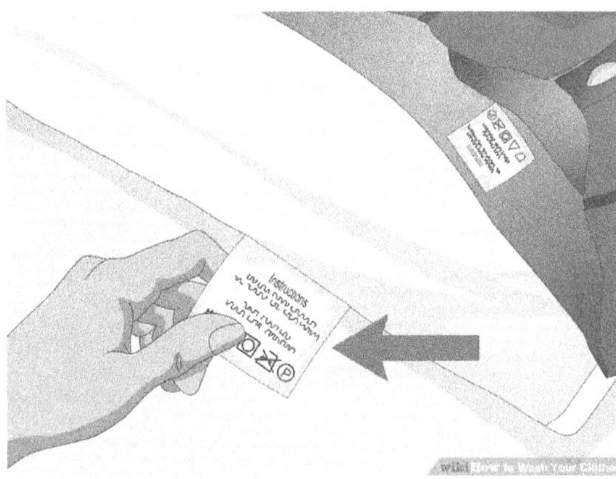

Label instructions. Image Source: WikiHow

Step 3: Loading

Now that you've sorted and checked labels, it's time to load the washing machine in the order you have sorted them. Do not overload the washing machine! Clothes need room to move around to get clean. Too much, and your clothes won't clean properly; too little, and you're wasting water and energy.

A good rule of thumb is to fill it about three-quarters full. After filling, add the right amount of detergent for your load. If you're unsure, the packaging usually provides guidance.

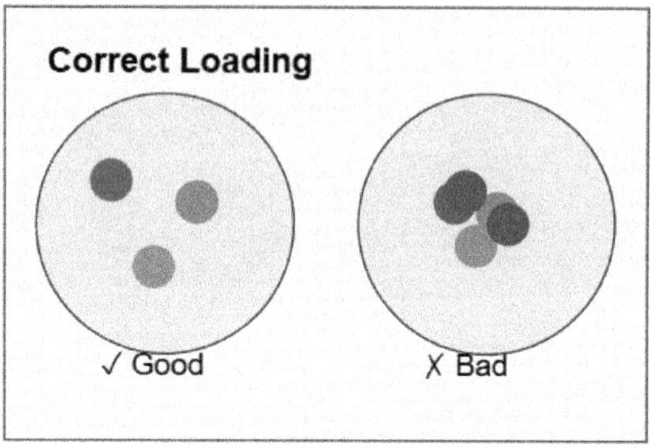

For clothes that might bleed:

- Wash them separately with cold water (hot water makes colors run faster - think of it like melting crayons!)
- Turn them inside out before washing

- Try using special "color catcher" sheets that trap loose dye in the wash.

- Add a cup of white vinegar to the wash or one-half cup of salt (sounds weird, but it helps lock in the color.)

Note: *Vinegar doesn't usually stain clothes, but it is acidic, so it's best not to pour it directly onto clothing without diluting it first. If your washing machine doesn't have a detergent compartment, mix ½ cup of vinegar with a cup of water before adding it to your laundry. Don't worry about the pungent smell—it washes out completely during the cycle, leaving your clothes crisp and vibrant.*

Open the door, add your detergent and close. Image Source: WikiHow

Step 4: Choose the Right Cycle

Select the washing cycle that suits your load best. Here's a quick guide to the primary washing cycles you'll find on most washing machines:

- **Normal:** This is for your everyday clothes that just need a good wash. It works great for cotton and durable fabrics.
- **Quick/Speed Wash:** When you need something cleaned fast, like a shirt for tomorrow, this setting does the trick in less time.
- **Heavy-duty:** Do you have really dirty clothes, like the clothes you wear for sports or towels? This cycle gives them extra cleaning power.
- **Permanent Press:** This cycle is suitable for clothes that you don't want to get wrinkled, like dress shirts or pants.
- **Delicate/Wool:** Use this gentle setting for fragile clothes like silk or special items that need extra care.

- **Bulky/Sheets:** If you're washing big stuff like blankets or comforters, this setting helps ensure they get cleaned well without getting stuck.

- **Whites:** This one's for your white clothes that need a deeper clean to stay bright and fresh.

- **Colors:** Use this for your colorful clothes to prevent fading and dullness.

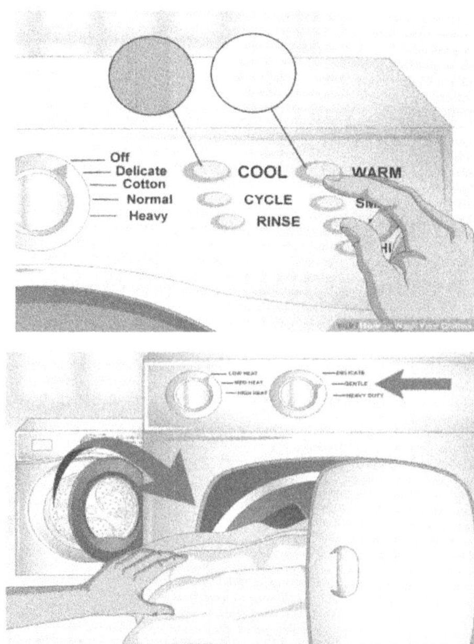

Choose based on explained criteria above. Image Source: WikiHow

Step 5: Drying

The best part about using a washing machine is that many washing machines will wash and spin your clothes all in one go. See how easy it is? It makes you wonder why you were ever lazy about doing your laundry in the first place. But here's the thing: even though the machine spins the clothes, sometimes it doesn't completely dry them. If you leave damp clothes sitting around, they might start to smell.

To avoid this, you have a couple of options. First, you can air-dry your clothes. This means hanging them up to dry, either on hangers in your closet or on a clothesline outside if the weather is nice. Air drying allows the moisture to evaporate naturally, leaving your clothes fresh and ready to wear. Alternatively, if your clothes are just slightly damp, you can iron them right after they're dry enough.

Step 6: Ironing

Before you even think about touching that iron, let's talk safety:

- **ALWAYS** have an adult nearby when you're learning to iron
- Remember: An iron can get as hot as an oven! It can seriously burn you
- Never touch the metal plate of the iron to check if it's hot
- Keep the cord away from the edges of the ironing board where it could be pulled
- If you need to adjust clothes, use the non-iron end or wait until the iron is upright
- Never leave a hot iron face-down on any surface – always use the heel rest
- If you feel unsure about anything, STOP and ask an adult for help
- Have an adult check your setup before you begin
- Make sure you're wearing appropriate clothes (no loose sleeves that could touch the iron)

- Keep a clear space around your ironing area – no toys or distractions!
- Always iron on a proper ironing board or heat-resistant surface
- Have a grown-up show you how to fill the water tank if you're using steam

An iron on its heel. Image source: iStock

Now that you are clear on safety, you should know that not all clothes need ironing. To be sure, check the care label of the clothing to see if ironing is necessary.

Ironing your clothes may appear intimidating at first, but once you know the basics, it's a straightforward task.

First, gather your supplies: an iron, an ironing board (or find a flat surface), and water if your iron has a steam function. Before you start, check the care labels on your clothes to determine the appropriate heat setting for the fabric.

Once you've set up your ironing board in a comfortable spot and plugged in the iron, adjust the temperature according to the fabric type. For instance, cotton typically requires a high setting, while silk needs low heat. If your iron has a steam function, fill the reservoir with water to help remove wrinkles more effectively.

For shirts, start with the collar and cuffs, laying them flat on the ironing board. Press the iron gently, moving from the edges towards the center to avoid creases. Then, move to the sleeves and body of the shirt, smoothing out any wrinkles with even strokes. If you're ironing pants, focus on the waistband first and then work down the legs, ensuring the seams remain sharp.

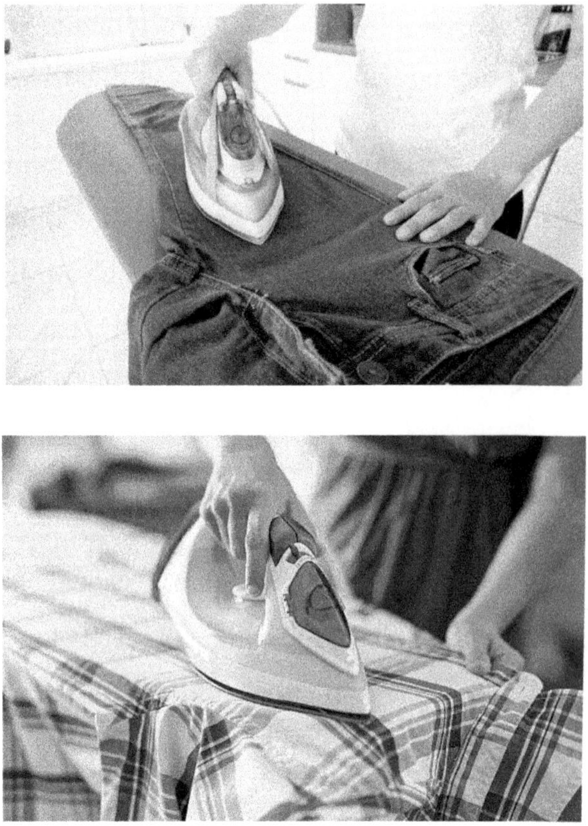

Proper ironing on an ironing board. Image source: iStock

Once you've finished ironing, hang your clothes on a hanger or lay them flat to cool, helping to set the pressed shape. When you're done, remember to turn off and unplug the iron and allow it to cool down before storing it away.

After Ironing Safety Checklist:

- Turn off the iron immediately when you're done
- Unplug it right away – don't wait!
- Place the iron upright on its heel and let it cool completely
- Keep everyone (especially younger siblings) away while it's cooling
- Never wrap the cord around a hot iron
- Wait until the iron is completely cool before putting it away
- Keep the iron and cord stored high up, out of reach of smaller children

Pro Tip: Keep a list of these safety rules near your ironing area until you know them by heart. Safety isn't just a rule – it's the coolest way to iron!

Step 7: Fold and Put Away

After ironing, fold your clothes and put them away. This is where many people falter—don't let clean clothes pile up on your chair or bed! Take the extra few minutes to put everything in its place.

Here's the fastest way to fold a t-shirt that actually works:

- Lay the t-shirt face-down on a flat surface
- Fold each side in about 3 inches
- Fold the bottom up to meet the collar
- Fold in half again

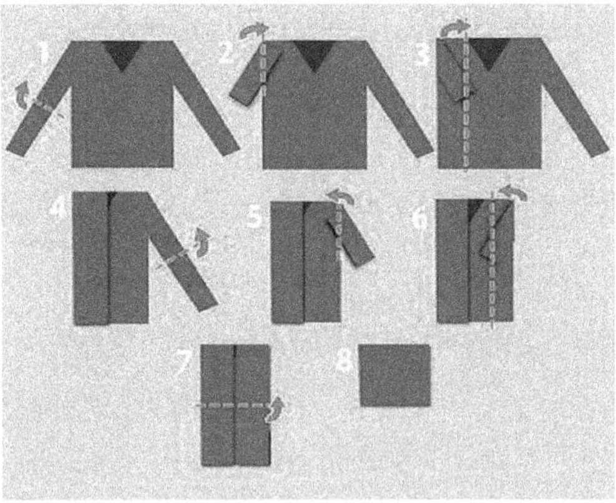

How to fold a shirt. Image source: Mail Online

For Pants:

1. Lay pants flat on a surface

2. Match the legs together, lining up the seams

3. Fold in half lengthwise

4. Fold the bottom up to the waistband

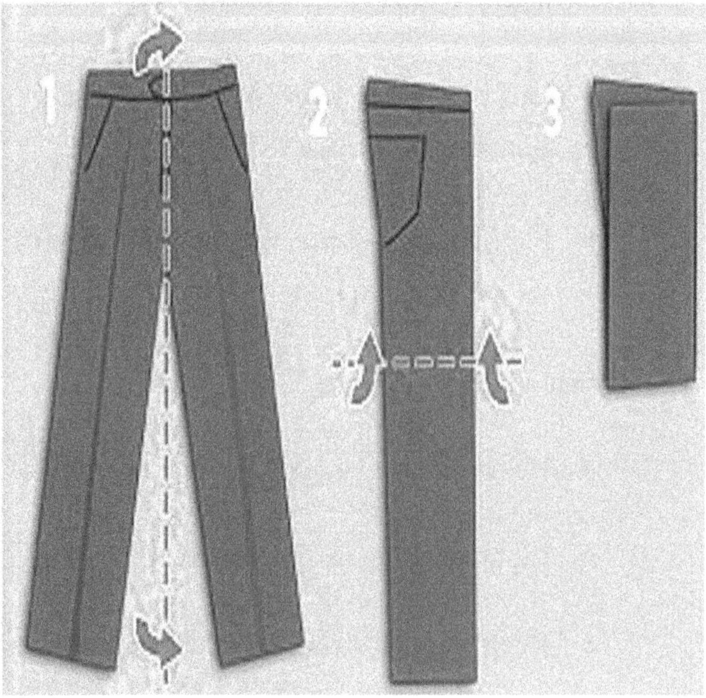

How to fold pants. Image source: Mail Online

Pro Tips:

- Fold right after the clothes are dry to avoid wrinkles
- Store folded clothes vertically in drawers (like files in a cabinet) so you can see everything at once
- Use drawer dividers to keep different types of clothes separate
- Don't overstuff drawers - this will mess up your folding
- For hanging clothes, use the same type of hangers for a cleaner look

Storage Rules:

- Heavy items like jeans go at the bottom of stacks
- Lightweight items like t-shirts go on top
- Keep similar items together (all t-shirts in one drawer, all pants in another)

- Store seasonal clothes (like winter sweaters) in separate containers when not in use

Handwashing

Some clothes are too delicate for the washing machine and need special care. Delicate clothing is made from soft, fragile fabrics that can easily get damaged in a washing machine or dryer. Think of materials like silk, satin, lace, or thin, see-through fabrics like chiffon. You'll often find care labels on these items that say things like "hand-wash only" or "dry clean recommended."

Some examples of delicate clothing include fancy underwear, clothes with beads or sequins. Sweaters made from special wools, like cashmere, are also delicate because they can shrink or lose their shape in a machine. Even soft, stretchy sweaters, workout clothes and ties should be hand-washed.

What You'll Need:

- A clean sink or wash basin
- Gentle detergent

- Clean white towels
- Cool or lukewarm water
- A soft surface to lay items flat

Step-by-Step Guide:

Step 1: Prep Time!

Check the care label first! Look for the little hand symbol Fill your sink or wash basin with cool or lukewarm water (not hot!). Add a small amount of gentle detergent (just a teaspoon is enough)

Step 2: The Gentle Dip

Submerge your item completely in the water. DON'T twist, wring, or stretch the fabric. Instead, gently squeeze the soapy water through the fabric. Think of it like giving your clothes a gentle massage! Pay extra attention to any spots that got dirty. Let it soak for about 5 minutes if it's really dirty.

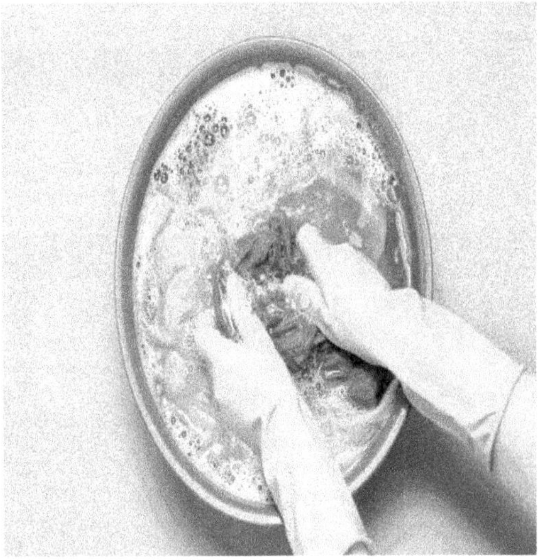

Gentle washing. Image source: iStock

Step 3: Rinsing

Drain the soapy water. Fill the sink with clean, cool water. Gently squeeze the fabric to remove soap. If water becomes too soapy, drain again and fill with clean water. Keep rinsing until the water runs clear (no more bubbles!) and no slippery feeling in the fabric.

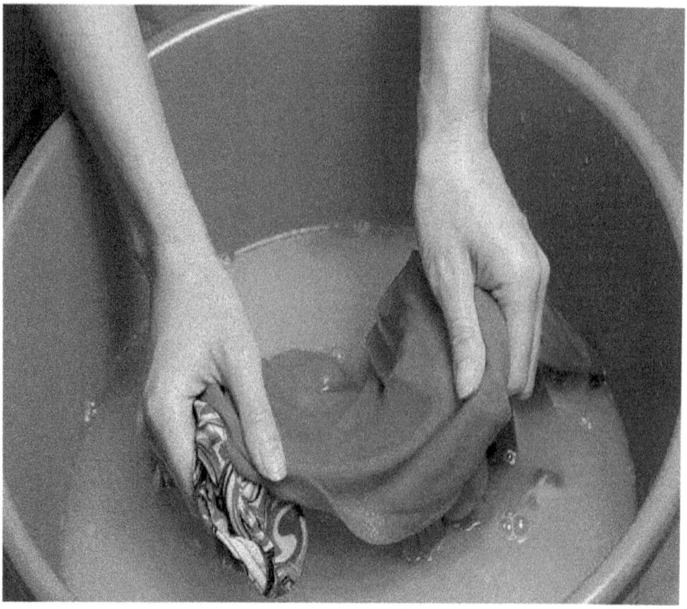

Rinsing until no bubbles are seen. Image source: iStock

Step 4: Drying

Never twist or wring the water out – this can stretch your clothes. Instead, press the water out gently with clean towels. Lay the item flat on a fresh, dry towel. Roll the towel and garment together and press gently to remove water. Unroll and move to a dry towel repeating the process of removing water. Finally, lay the garment flat and reshape to its original form (this is super important!) to air dry.

Pro Tips:

- If you're not sure about something, ask an adult to help
- Never use hot water – it can shrink or damage delicate clothes
- Don't hang wet sweaters – they'll stretch out of shape
- Use white towels to avoid color transfer

Warning Signs to Watch For:

- If the water turns very dark
- If you see the color running
- If you notice any tears or loose threads STOP and ask for help!

Clothes Label instructions. Image source: iStock

Now that you know the basics, here are some practical tips to make laundry feel less daunting:

- **Create a Laundry Schedule:** Set aside a specific day each week for laundry. This routine will help prevent overwhelming piles from accumulating and keep your wardrobe fresh.

- **Make it Fun:** Turn laundry day into an enjoyable experience! Play your favorite music or listen to an audiobook while you sort and fold. You might find that time flies by.

- **Use Laundry Baskets:** Invest in laundry baskets for sorting. Having designated spaces for dirty clothes will encourage you to put items away instead of letting them pile up.

- **Ask for Help if Needed:** If you ever feel uncertain about how to handle a specific garment or laundry task, don't hesitate to ask a parent or older sibling for guidance. Learning is all about asking questions!

- **Celebrate Small Wins:** After finishing a load of laundry, take a moment to pat yourself on the back. Acknowledge the hard work you've put in—after all, you've just taken care of your clothes and made your life a little easier!

Basic Cooking Skills

Have you ever wondered how the delicious meals you enjoy are prepared? You might think cooking is something only adults do, but let me tell you: you are not too young to know how to cook! In fact, many of the world's best chefs started cooking at a young age. For example, Gordon Ramsay began showing interest in cooking as a teenager and enrolled in hotel management school at just 19. Martin Yan started at age 12, working in his uncle's Chinese restaurant. Stuart O'Keeffe was only seven when he became a "right handy sous-chef" in his family kitchen, helping his mother and aunt prepare pies and pastries. So, who knows? You could be the next culinary superstar, but you might be stifling that talent by not even trying!

Cooking is more than just turning on the stove and following a recipe. It's about understanding what you want to eat, planning your meals, shopping for the right ingredients, and finally, transforming those ingredients into something delicious.

Let's start by talking about planning. Take a moment to jot down a few meals you'd like to try. For instance, maybe you're interested in making a tasty omelet, a fresh salad, or even a simple pasta dish. Writing down your ideas not only helps you remember what you want to make but also guides your shopping list.

Once you have your meal ideas, you make a grocery list. Think about the ingredients you'll need for each dish. For an omelet, you'll need eggs, cheese, and some veggies like bell peppers or spinach. If you plan to make a salad, jot down ingredients like lettuce, tomatoes, and your favorite dressing. This list will be your reminder when you hit the grocery store, ensuring you don't forget anything important.

Grocery Shopping

When you think about grocery shopping, you might picture your parents loading the cart with stuff while you follow along, hoping to sneak in a snack or two. But this time around, you are the one pushing the cart, confidently choosing the ingredients for your own meals.

Once you arrive at the store, stick to your list. When picking fresh produce, look for vibrant colors and firm textures. For example, ripe tomatoes should be bright red and slightly soft but not mushy. If you're buying meat or dairy, check expiration dates to ensure you're getting the freshest products.

Pro-tip: While shopping, keep an eye out for sales or discounts. If you see a good deal on an item you need, buy it. But don't forget to check expiry dates and freshness of the item.

Let's explore a few easy dishes you can make, along with a grocery list and tips on shopping for them.

Omelets

- **Eggs:** Look for large eggs in the dairy section. Check the expiration date to ensure they're fresh.

- **Cheese:** You can choose your favorite type, like cheddar or mozzarella. Find it in the dairy aisle.

- **Vegetables:** Common choices include bell peppers, spinach, and onions. From the produce section, choose fresh, vibrant vegetables. They should feel firm and have no bruises. If they're wilted or mushy, it's better to skip them.

Salad

- **Lettuce or Mixed Greens:** Look for crisp, bright greens in the produce section. You can choose romaine, iceberg, or a bag of pre-washed mixed greens.

- **Tomatoes:** Pick plump, red tomatoes. Cherry tomatoes are also a great option since they're bite-sized and sweet.

- **Cucumbers:** Choose a firm cucumber. You can slice it into rounds or spears for crunch.

- **Carrots:** You can peel and slice baby carrots or regular carrots, which add a nice crunch and sweetness.

- **Dressing:** You can choose a store-bought dressing or make your own with olive oil and vinegar.

Now, let's say you've gathered all your ingredients. It's time to head home and dive into the cooking process!

Cooking Simple Recipes

Cooking begins with knowing how to prepare simple recipes. Starting with a few foundational dishes can build your confidence and encourage you to experiment in the kitchen. The dishes you went grocery shopping for above are great dishes to start with.

Omelet Recipe

Ingredients:

- 2 large eggs
- 2 tablespoons milk
- 1/4 cup shredded cheese
- 1/4 cup diced vegetables (bell peppers, onions, spinach, etc.)
- 1 tablespoon butter or oil
- Salt and pepper to taste

Instructions:

1. Wash your hands to make sure they're clean. Gather all your ingredients and tools. You will need a bowl, a whisk or fork, a non-stick frying pan, and a spatula (the flat tool for flipping).

2. Take your vegetables, wash them under running water, and then chop them into small pieces. You want them to be bite-sized, so they cook quickly and fit nicely in your omelet. Ask an adult to help if you need it!

3. Crack the eggs into the bowl—be careful not to get any shells in there! Add the milk, a pinch of salt, and a little pepper. Using a whisk or fork, beat the eggs and milk together until they are mixed well and look a bit frothy.

4. Put your pan on the stove and turn the heat to medium. Add the butter or oil. Wait for it to melt and get a little bubbly. This will help the omelet not stick to the pan.

5. Once the butter is melted, add the chopped vegetables to the pan. Cook them for about 1-2 minutes, stirring occasionally, until they are soft.

6. Carefully pour the egg mixture over the cooked vegetables in the skillet. Make sure the eggs cover the veggies evenly. Let it cook for about 1-2 minutes. You'll see the edges starting to set.

7. Sprinkle the shredded cheese over one-half of the omelet. This will melt beautifully as the eggs continue to cook.

8. Using your spatula, gently fold the omelet in half so the cheese is on the inside. Cook for another minute or so until the cheese melts and the eggs are fully cooked.

9. Carefully slide the omelet onto a plate. If you like, you can sprinkle some extra cheese or herbs on top. If you want to share, cut it in half, or just dig in!

Simple Salad Recipe

Ingredients:

- 2 cups mixed greens or lettuce (like romaine or spinach)

- 1/2 medium tomato (diced)

- 1/4 cucumber (sliced)
- 1 tablespoon salad dressing (like ranch, balsamic vinaigrette, or Italian)
- Optional: Croutons (small toasted bread pieces) or seeds for topping

Instructions:

1. Start by washing your hands (as always) to keep everything clean.
2. Rinse the mixed greens under cold water and let them dry in a salad spinner or on a clean paper towel. Wash the tomato and cut it into small pieces (ask an adult for help with this!). Slice the cucumber into thin rounds.
3. In a large bowl, add the mixed greens first. Then, add the diced tomato and cucumber slices.
4. Drizzle the salad dressing over the top. Start with a little; you can always add more later!

5. Use two forks or your clean hands to toss the salad gently. This means mixing it all together so the dressing coats everything evenly.

6. If you want some extra crunch, sprinkle croutons or seeds on top. You can eat it right away or keep it in the fridge for a little while.

Cooking is all about having fun, experimenting, and trying new things. You might not get it perfect every time, but that's part of the learning process! The more you practice, the better you'll become in the kitchen. Here are a few more easy recipes that you can try out.

Scrambled Eggs Recipe

Ingredients:

- 2 large eggs
- 2 tablespoons milk (optional for creaminess)
- Salt and pepper to taste
- 1 tablespoon butter or oil

- Optional add-ins: shredded cheese, diced vegetables (like bell peppers, onions, or spinach), or herbs (like chives or parsley)

Instructions:

1. Crack the eggs into a bowl. If you're using milk, add it to the eggs. This will make your scrambled eggs a bit creamier.

2. Beat the eggs with a fork or whisk until the yolks and whites are fully combined. Add a pinch of salt and pepper to taste. If you're adding cheese or vegetables, have them ready.

3. Place a non-stick pan on the stove over medium heat and add the butter or oil. Allow it to melt and coat the bottom of the pan.

4. Once the butter is melted and bubbling slightly, pour the egg mixture into the pan. Let it sit for a moment until the edges start to set.

5. Use a spatula to gently stir the eggs, pushing them from the edges toward the center. Continue to cook, stirring

occasionally, until the eggs are mostly set but still slightly runny. This usually takes about 2-3 minutes.

6. If you're adding cheese, vegetables, or herbs, sprinkle them on top when the eggs are almost done cooking. Give everything a quick stir to mix it in.

7. Remove the pan from the heat when the eggs are still slightly soft and creamy (they will continue to cook off the heat).

8. Transfer the scrambled eggs to a plate and enjoy them warm. You can serve them on their own or with toast!

How to Brew Tea

Ingredients:

- 1 tea bag or 1 teaspoon of loose-leaf tea (loose-leaf tea is a tea that does not come prepackaged in tea bags)

- 1 cup of water

- Optional: milk, lemon, honey, or sugar for flavoring

Instructions:

1. Start by boiling water. You can use a kettle or a saucepan on the stove. If you're using an electric kettle, wait for it to beep when the water is ready.

2. If you're using a tea bag, simply place it in your cup or mug. If you're using loose-leaf tea, you might want to use a tea infuser or strainer to make it easier to remove the leaves later.

3. Once the water reaches a boil, carefully pour it over the tea bag or loose leaves in your cup.

4. Allow the tea to steep (soak) for about 3-5 minutes, depending on how strong you like your tea. Black tea typically requires about 3-5 minutes, while green tea usually needs only 2-3 minutes.

5. After the steeping time, remove the tea bag or strain the loose leaves from the cup.

6. If you like, you can enhance the flavor of your tea by adding a splash of milk, a slice of lemon, or a spoonful of honey or sugar.

7. Give your tea a gentle stir to mix in any added ingredients, and then enjoy it while it's warm!

Healthy Eating

When you step into the kitchen, it's important to understand the ingredients you're working with. You might have heard terms like saturated and unsaturated fats, but what do they really mean?

Saturated fats are typically solid at room temperature and are found in foods like butter, cheese, and red meat. While these fats can be tasty, consuming too much isn't the best for your health. Why? Because consuming a lot of saturated fats can lead to high cholesterol levels in your blood, which might increase your risk of heart problems later in life. Think of your arteries (the vessels or tubes that carry blood around your body) as roads. If there's too much "traffic" (or cholesterol) on those roads, it can cause blockages that slow everything down.

Unsaturated fats are usually liquid at room temperature and come from sources like olive oil, avocados, and nuts. These are the healthier choices because they help lower bad cholesterol levels in your blood. They're like the good guys who help keep your "roads" clear! Eating unsaturated fats in moderation can support your heart health and overall well-being.

When cooking, try to use unsaturated fats whenever possible. For example, instead of cooking with butter, consider olive oil or avocado oil. If you're having a sandwich, add slices of avocado instead of mayonnaise for a creamy texture without the unhealthy fats. These options not only enhance the flavor of your meals but also contribute positively to your health.

Refined and Processed Food

These terms can be a bit confusing, so let's break them down. Refined foods undergo a process that removes some of their natural nutrients. A good example is white bread, which is made from refined flour. This type of flour has had the fiber and vitamins removed, making it less nutritious than whole grain bread, which keeps all the good stuff. Processed foods are those that have been altered from their original form. This can include things like frozen dinners, snacks, and sugary cereals. While they may be convenient and quick to prepare, many processed foods contain high levels of salt, sugar, and unhealthy fats, which aren't great for your body.

So, while it's okay to enjoy these foods occasionally, focusing on whole, unprocessed foods is a healthier choice. Whole foods are those that are close to their natural state—like fresh fruits, vegetables, whole grains, and lean proteins. For example, when you think of a healthy snack, reaching for an apple or a handful of almonds is a better option than grabbing a bag of chips.

Lean meat refers to cuts of meat that have less fat compared to other types. Good examples include chicken breast, turkey, and certain cuts of beef, like sirloin or tenderloin. Lean meats are great options because they provide protein without a lot of extra fat, making them a healthier choice for your meals.

An example of a healthy cooking process is making a stir-fry. You might use a mix of bright bell peppers, crunchy broccoli, and lean chicken or tofu sautéed in a little olive oil. This combination not only tastes delicious but also provides your body with important nutrients.

Kitchen Safety

Now that you're excited about cooking and have learned about fats and healthy eating let's talk about something equally important: kitchen safety! Cooking can be a blast, but it's essential to stay safe while you whip up those delicious meals. Think of the kitchen as your playground—full of fun and creativity, but also a place where you need to be aware of your surroundings and the tools you're using. After all, the last thing you want is to turn your cooking adventure into a kitchen catastrophe!

8 Kitchen Safety Tips for You

1. Always use a cutting board when chopping vegetables or preparing food. This protects your countertops and keeps your knife from getting dull.

2. When using knives, remember to keep your fingers tucked in. This action protects your fingers and gives you better control of what you're cutting.

3. If you're cooking on the stove, make sure pot handles are turned inward, away from the edge. This prevents

someone from accidentally knocking them over while moving around the kitchen.

4. Always use oven mitts when handling hot cookware. They may seem like a small detail, but they can save you from burns!

5. Never leave cooking food unattended, especially if you're using high heat. If you need to step away, turn off the stove or ask someone to watch it for you.

6. If you spill something, clean it up right away. Slipping on a wet floor can lead to injuries, so keep your cooking space tidy!

7. Take a moment to familiarize yourself with your kitchen tools. Whether it's a blender, food processor, or mixer, knowing how to operate them safely will make your cooking experience much smoother.

8. When handling sharp utensils, be mindful of where your hands are and how you're moving. If you drop something, let it fall—don't try to catch it mid-air!

Finally, don't forget about the importance of cleaning up after cooking. Just as you learned earlier about maintaining a tidy space, a clean kitchen is vital for a positive and joyous cooking experience. After you've enjoyed your meal, take a few minutes to wash your dishes, wipe down the counters, and put away any leftover ingredients. This routine keeps your kitchen organized and prepares you for your next cooking adventure.

Basic First Aid

Ever scraped your knee playing basketball? Cut your finger while building something? Or accidentally touched something hot? These things happen to everyone. Knowing basic first aid means you can handle these situations calmly and safely. Let's learn the right way to deal with common injuries.

Immediate Action for Cuts

If you get a cut that's bleeding heavily, immediately call the emergency line for help or find an adult or older family member for help. Right before they arrive or if no older person is present, here's what you should do.

If the Cut is Bleeding Heavily:

1. Stop what you're doing and turn off any equipment or heat sources

2. Check if anything is stuck in the wound

   If nothing is stuck: Press firmly with a clean cloth or towel

   If something is stuck: Press on both sides of the object, don't remove it

3. For hand or arm cuts, raise your arm high above your head. Keep pressing on the wound

4. For leg cuts, lie down. Raise your leg higher than your heart and keep pressing on the wound.

5. Press firmly for 10 minutes without lifting to check

6. If blood soaks through, add another cloth on top - don't remove the first one

7. Keep pressing for another 10 minutes.

For Small Cuts (Once Bleeding Has Slowed)

1. Clean the wound by running it under tap water
2. Clean the skin around the cut with soap and water or antiseptic but carefully so it doesn't touch the cut itself.
3. Pat the area dry with a clean cloth or paper towel
4. Apply an antiseptic cream from the medical cupboard.
5. Cover with a bandage or plaster

Immediate Actions for Minor Burns

If you get burnt by flames, immediately call the emergency line for help or find an adult or older family member for help. Right before they arrive or if no older person is present, here's what you should do.

1. Hold burnt area under cool (not cold) running water for 10 minutes

   For face burns: apply a cool, wet clean cloth

   For mouth burns from hot food/drinks: Put a single ice cube in your mouth and let it slowly melt or place 15 to 20 granules of sugar in the mouth and suck on it. Remove the ice after a few minutes

2. Quickly but carefully remove any tight items like rings, watches, tight sleeves. Do this right away before swelling starts. If item is stuck, wait for medical help

3. Once the burnt area has cooled down, apply either aloe vera lotion, or cocoa butter. Never use butter, oil, ice, toothpaste or kitchen ingredients

4. Use a clean, sterile bandage to wrap the burn loosely to avoid pressure

5. Don't break any forming/formed blisters

After treatment, always remember to change bandages daily or when dirty and make sure you are keeping the area clean and dry and free from infection.

Warning Signs of infection:

- Increased redness
- Swelling
- Warm to touch

- Pus or odd smell

Important Tips

- Know where first aid supplies are kept at home and school
- Keep emergency numbers in your phone
- Have your parent/guardian's phone number easily accessible
- Memories your home address/note it down in your diary or mobile phone in case you need to call for help

Your safety comes first. If you're unsure about how serious an injury is, it's better to call for help than to wait.

PRACTICAL EXERCISE 2

1 - Room Organization Challenge

Duration: 30 minutes

Materials Needed: Timer, storage containers/boxes, trash bag

- Set timer for 5 minutes to assess your room
- Identify 3 main problem areas
- Sort items into categories:
    - Keep (in regular use)
    - Store (seasonal/occasional use)
    - Donate/Sell
    - Trash
- Create designated spaces for frequently used items
- Test your organization by timing how long it takes to find 5 specific items

2 - Daily Clean-Up Routine Challenge

Morning Checklist:

- Make bed immediately after waking
- Put night clothes away

- Clear any dishes/trash from bedroom
- Open windows for 5 minutes to air out room

Evening Checklist:

- Clear floor of any items
- Return items to designated spots
- Quick 5-minute desk organization
- Prepare clothes for tomorrow

Track Your Progress: Create a week-long chart marking each completed task. Aim for consistency rather than perfection!

3 - Folding Practice Challenge

Materials Needed: Various clothing types

Skills Checklist: Practice folding each type 3 times:

- T-shirts
- Pants/jeans
- Towels
- Sheets
- Underwear
- Socks (matching pairs)

Time yourself: Try to improve speed while maintaining neatness

4 - Speed Cleaning Challenge

Time yourself completing these tasks:

- Making bed (target: under 3 minutes)
- Desk organization (target: under 5 minutes)
- Floor cleanup (target: under 10 minutes)

Progress Journal

Keep track of your progress with these prompts:

1. What was the most challenging task today?
2. Which skill showed the most improvement?
3. What could you do differently next time?
4. How has mastering these skills made your daily life easier?

Achievement Levels

Novice Cleaner

- *Completed daily checklists for one week*
- *Mastered basic bed-making*
- *Successfully sort one load of laundry*

Intermediate Organizer

- *Maintained room organization for two weeks*
- *Perfected folding techniques for all basic items*
- *Created and followed a cleaning schedule*

Advanced Domestic Master

- *Created efficient storage solutions*
- *Handled all laundry tasks alone*
- *Taught these basic skills to someone else*

“It doesn’t matter what others are doing - what matters is what you are doing”

- *Weareteachers*

SKILL 3: DEVELOPING YOUR PERSONALITY

Have you ever thought about what makes *you*—you? You walk into a room filled with people. Some are laughing and chatting, while others are quiet, looking around. What makes the difference? It often comes down to personality—who is more social and friendly—and the choices people make every day, whether to start a conversation or just remain on their own.

Your personality isn't only about what you like or dislike; it's about how you face challenges, take charge of your life, and handle everyday situations. Every time you encounter a challenge, you have a chance to grow. Each decision you make shapes who you are, and how you respond to different situations builds your character. In this chapter, we'll explore how accepting responsibility, understanding yourself and developing critical thinking skills can help you become the best version of yourself.

Accepting Responsibility and Accountability

Jake had always been the fun-loving guy in his friend group. One Friday afternoon, he was tasked with bringing snacks for their movie night. Excited about the gathering, he promised his friends, "Don't worry, I've got it covered!" But as the day went on, Jake got distracted by a new video game. When the time came to head over to his friend's house, he realized he hadn't picked up anything for the night. Grabbing something from the fridge was the next option; the snacks wouldn't be as much, but they'd be better than nothing.

As he headed downstairs, he received a call from Gina, his crush. Suddenly, all thoughts of snacks slipped from his mind. They chatted about everything—school, their favorite shows, and even made plans for the weekend. The conversation lasted the entire journey to his friend's house, and in the excitement of talking to Gina, Jake completely forgot to stop by the store that was always open midway to his friend's place.

As they settled in for the movie, his friends turned to him, expecting a spread of snacks. Instead, they found Jake empty-handed. “I forgot,” he muttered, shrugging his shoulders. His friends were disappointed, but Jake shrugged it off, thinking, “It’s not a big deal. They’ll get over it.” Unfortunately for him, this wasn’t the first time he had made promises he didn’t keep.

This moment is a classic example of how avoiding responsibility can lead to negative consequences. When Jake failed to bring the snacks, it wasn’t just about the food. His friends felt let down, and that feeling lingered. They started to see Jake as someone who didn’t take his commitments seriously. Over time, this pattern of behavior watered their trust in him. They would think twice before relying on him for anything important.

So, what does it mean to accept responsibility and accountability?

Responsibility is about owning up to your actions and their consequences. It means recognizing that you have a role in what happens in your life. In Jake's case, he had a responsibility to follow through on his promise to bring snacks. When he neglected this duty, he not only disappointed his friends but also missed out on an opportunity to learn from his mistake.

Accountability, on the other hand, is being willing to accept the results of your actions. You're ready to face the consequences of what you've done. Think of accountability as a mirror. When you look into it, you see your actions reflected back at you—good or bad. When Jake looked in that mirror, he could have seen a chance to grow, but he ignored it.

Accepting accountability means being honest with yourself and others about your actions, whether they are positive or negative. It's about saying, "I messed up, and I'll do better next time." In Jake's situation, he could have acknowledged his mistake, apologized to his friends, and promised to make it up to them. This honesty can go a long way in building trust with your friends and family. Instead, he chose to downplay the importance of his responsibility, which led to a loss of trust among his friends.

To help you understand this concept further, let's look at another story—about a boy named Marcus. Marcus was known for being late to school. He would often miss the bus, and instead of finding a solution, he would blame everything around him: the weather, his alarm clock, or even his dog. But one day, Marcus's mom spoke with him, and he realized that his actions were the real problem.

That morning, Marcus decided to take responsibility. He set his alarm earlier and laid out his clothes the night before. Marcus felt a great sense of accomplishment when he woke up on time and caught the bus. It was more than just being on time for him; he felt proud because it was the first time he had taken charge of his morning routine in a long while. Instead of pointing fingers, he acknowledged that he could change his situation with better planning.

Accepting responsibility and accountability in your life isn't just about the big moments; it's about your little choices every day. Whether it's helping out with chores at home, completing your homework on time, or keeping promises to friends, each action you take shapes your character. Being responsible doesn't mean you won't make mistakes; it means you're willing to learn from them and take steps to improve.

Now that you understand responsibility and accountability, how can you apply these concepts in your daily life?

Start Small

If you struggle with responsibility, begin by focusing on small tasks. For example, make your bed every morning or complete your homework before doing any other leisure activity. You build a foundation for larger responsibilities when you consistently complete these small tasks.

Set Reminders

Use your phone or a sticky note to remind yourself of important tasks. Whether it's taking out the trash or studying for a test, reminders help you stay on track. This simple tool can keep you accountable and ensure you don't forget your commitments.

Learn from Mistakes

Everyone makes mistakes; it's a part of growing up. Instead of dwelling on what went wrong, focus on what you can learn from the experience. Ask yourself, "What will I do differently next time?" This reflection helps you grow and avoid making the same mistake again.

Communicate Openly

If you're unable to meet a responsibility, be honest with those affected. For instance, if you can't bring snacks like Jake, tell your friends beforehand. They'll appreciate your honesty and be more understanding.

Make a Commitment

After accepting responsibility, commit to making it a priority. Tell yourself, "I will follow through on this," and hold yourself accountable. You can also share your goals with a friend or family member who can help keep you on track.

Reflective Question

Think about the responsibilities in your life. What's one thing you can take charge of this week, whether at home or school? How will you make sure you follow through?

Understanding Yourself

The first step to growing as a person is getting to know who you are. This means looking inside yourself to build what is called self-esteem and self-awareness.

Self-Esteem: Feeling Good About Yourself

Self-esteem is all about how much you love yourself and how much you believe in what you can do. It's like having an inner hype man that gives you the courage to take on challenges.

When your self-esteem is high, you feel unstoppable and without anyone telling you, you know that you deserve love and respect just for being you. But if your self-esteem is low, it can feel like there's a rain cloud over your head, making you feel unsure or scared about the things you can do.

Now, what all of this simply means is that if you have self-esteem, you have high confidence, like that popular guy at your school. You know the one – maybe he's the star quarterback everyone cheers for, or the guy who gets all the attention, or the one with the expensive clothes and latest gadgets. But here's the thing: his confidence might just come from having all that stuff handed to him.

Real self-esteem? That's something different. It's about being confident in yourself even when you don't have all those advantages. It doesn't matter if you're not the best-looking, the most athletic, or the richest guy in school. True self-esteem comes from inside you, not from what others think or what stuff you own.

But here's something you need to watch out for: there's a thin line between having solid self-esteem and being straight-up arrogant and being confident in yourself? That's cool. Acting like you're better than everyone else? Not cool at all. Real confidence doesn't mean putting others down to lift yourself up - trust me, that's not a good look.

Now, let's break this down in a way that'll make sense in your everyday life. You ace that math test you studied hard for. If you're confident, you feel good about it because you know you put in the work. You might even help your friends study for the next one. But if you're arrogant? You're the guy walking around saying stuff like "Did you guys seriously find that test hard? It was so easy!" I am sure you know that nobody likes that guy.

Or maybe you score the winning point in a game. Confidence is celebrating with your team because you all worked together to make it happen. Arrogance is going on social media to brag about how you "carried the whole team." Big difference.

The funny thing is, the most genuinely confident people you'll meet are often the quietest about their achievements. They don't need to shove their success in everyone's face because they're secure enough in themselves not to need constant validation.

So, here's the real talk: you can be confident without being arrogant, proud without being a "jerk." This is the type of confidence people respect way more than arrogant showboating. It's about knowing your worthwhile still being the kind of guy others want to hang out with.

Self-Awareness: Knowing Who You Are

Now, you know your phone has settings and you need to figure out how to make it work the best for you. Well, you've got settings too. Self-awareness is about getting into those settings and understanding what makes you tick.

Think about it - what gets you hyped? What makes you mad? What are you actually into, not just what your friends are into? That's the start of self-awareness. It's simply having the cheat codes to your own brain. When you do, you can easily make choices that feel right for you.

Self-awareness also means understanding your emotions. Sometimes, you might feel sad, angry, or worried, and that’s completely normal. What matters is figuring out why you feel that way and what you can do to feel better.

Another important part of self-awareness is understanding how you affect others. Everything you do is like throwing a stone in a pond—it creates ripples. The way you talk to people, the stuff you do, and even the way you carry yourself can either make people feel good or hurt. Being self-aware means understanding those ripples so you can build better relationships with the people around you.

Building self-esteem and being more self-aware go hand in hand. It’s all about understanding yourself better and supporting yourself in a positive way. Let's look at how you can do it:

Healthy Self-Talk

Sometimes negative thoughts sneak in and make you feel down. These thoughts might come from past experiences, someone's hurtful words, or fears about not being good enough.

The first step in dealing with these thoughts is to recognize them. Talk to yourself like you would talk to a friend—be kind and supportive. If you make a mistake, instead of saying, "I'm so bad at this," say, "Now I know what went wrong, and next time will be better." Or if you feel nervous, remind yourself, "It's okay to feel this way, and I'll do my best." This helps shift your mindset from being too hard on yourself to being more understanding and positive.

Question Negative Thoughts

When a negative thought pops into your head, question it. Ask yourself, "Is this really true, or am I just being too hard on myself?" Replace a thought like, "I'm terrible at everything," with something more balanced, like, "I'm still learning, and I'm getting better." It's like turning on a light in a dark room—suddenly, things don't seem as scary anymore.

Journaling

This is something that helps if you are able to look past the idea that it's a "girl's thing." Having records about you can help you be more self-aware. Grab a notebook (or your phone) and start writing stuff down. Not like "dear diary" stuff (unless that's your thing), but just notes about what's going on in your head. Write about your thoughts, feelings, and experiences. Ask yourself questions like, "What made me feel proud today?" What ticked me off? or "What do I want to achieve this week?" After a while, you'll start seeing patterns, and that's when things get interesting.

Talk Back to Your Inner Critic

Picture your negative thoughts as an annoying character, say Venom, one you can talk back to. You can even picture it as your annoying little sibling or that one teacher who always has something negative to say. Give it a name if you want. When it starts running its mouth like saying things like "You'll never be good at this," you can be like, "Not today, Bob." Sounds dumb, but it works. I mean not everyone starts out great—that's why we learn.

Physical Coping Tools

Sometimes your brain's just being too loud? That's when you gotten get physical. I don't mean picking fights – I'm talking about something that can help you move your body to connect your mind to something else. Stand like Superman for a minute or take on any power pose of your choice (when nobody's watching if you're feeling weird about it). Take some deep breaths. Go shoot some hoops. Your body and mind are connected – when you move your body, your mind follows.

Developing Positive Relationships

The people around you - your friends, your family - shape who you become more than you might realize. Every conversation, every move you make together, and every time they back you up (or let you down) affects how you think and who you'll turn out to be. These aren't just people you game with or sit next to at lunch. These connections can either hold you back or help you level up in life.

Building solid relationships isn't like following some random school formula. They also don't just happen by accident. They take understanding, effort, and sometimes getting out of your comfort zone. But here's why you should care: knowing how to build strong connections with people is a skill that'll take you places - whether that's making the team, landing that job you want, or just becoming someone people actually want to have around.

Let's break down how to build these connections the right way.

Your Squad

Real friendship isn't complicated, but it is rare. A solid friend is someone who has your back, keeps it real with you, and respects your boundaries. They hype you up when you're doing well and tell you straight when you're messing up. But you've got to know what's not okay too. If someone's always dragging you down, trying to run your life, or making you feel like you're not good enough - that's not a friend. Don't waste your time there.

Drama happens. That's just facts. Maybe you and your friend disagree about something, or there's some beef that needs sorting. What matters isn't that you never have conflicts - it's how you handle them. Sometimes you need to compromise. Sometimes you need to have uncomfortable conversations. The goal is finding solutions where you both feel respected and heard.

Making new friends can feel awkward, especially if you're not the most outgoing guy. But here's what works: find people who are into what you're into. Join that club, that team, or that group that does stuff you actually care about. When someone's talking about something they're passionate about, ask them about it. It's as simple as that. There's no need to fake it or try too hard. You’ll be surprised how often a simple conversation can turn into a lasting friendship.

The Home Team

Family is different. You don't choose them, but they're usually the ones who've been there from day one. But it’s still funny how miscommunication still happens. That’s why when things get tense at home (and they will), instead of getting mad or shutting down, good communication comes into play. Explain what's actually bothering you. "When this happens, it frustrates me. Can we talk about it?" This hits home differently than slamming doors or giving them the silent treatment.

Here's something you should always think about: everyone in your family is dealing with their own stuff. Your parents have their pressures, your siblings have their struggles. You don't have to agree with everything they do or say, but understanding where they're coming from makes life at home way easier. You also need to understand boundaries and respect them just like you’d want them to do the same for yourself, too.

It’s also a fantastic idea for families to keep some bonding time. Yes, everyone is busy, and stressed, doing their own thing. But making time to connect - whether it is watching the game together, grabbing food, or just talking about your day over dinner - that stuff matters. These moments build stronger connections between everyone, even if they seem small.

The skills you learn now about dealing with people - how to communicate clearly, handle disagreements, build trust - these aren't just "soft skills" or whatever. This is real stuff that'll matter in everything from sports teams to future jobs. Every solid relationship you build makes you stronger. You might mess up sometimes. That's normal. What matters is that you keep working at it, keep learning, and keep pushing yourself to build connections that actually mean something.

Critical Thinking and Problem Solving

There's this kid named Alex. One afternoon, Alex and his friends decided to have a basketball game at the park. They were super pumped, but when they got there, they realized something was missing—the basketball! Instead of sulking and calling it a day, Alex had a bright idea. He suggested they use a makeshift basketball. They could take an old backpack, stuff it with some clothes to make it round and use that instead. Sure, it wouldn't bounce like a real basketball, but it was better than nothing. They laughed as they played, and the makeshift ball ended up being a hit, turning the game into a fun memory.

This is a perfect example of using critical thinking to find a solution when things don't go as planned.

Critical thinking is all about looking at problems from different angles and coming up with solutions. It's like being a detective; you analyze the clues and conclude. Whether you're faced with a school project, a sports challenge, or even a tricky friendship situation, critical thinking allows you to figure things out logically and creatively.

So, what does it take to develop a solution-oriented mindset? It begins with understanding that challenges are opportunities for growth. Instead of seeing problems as roadblocks, think of them as puzzles waiting to be solved. The first step is to define the issue clearly. Ask yourself questions like, "What is happening?" and "Why is this a problem?" The clearer you are about the problem, the easier it will be to find a solution.

After identifying the problem, gather all the information you need to help solve it. This might mean talking to someone who has experienced a similar issue or doing a little research online. For example, if you're having trouble with math homework, you can reach out to a friend who understands the subject better.

Once you have all the information, it's time to brainstorm possible solutions. This means letting your imagination run wild. Think of all the possible solutions, even the silly ones. Sometimes, the craziest ideas can lead to the best solutions. For example, if you're struggling to finish a project on time, think about all your options: Can you ask for an extension? Can you break the project into smaller tasks and work on it a little each day? Could you team up with a classmate for help?

After brainstorming, take a closer look at each solution. Consider the pros and cons of each option. Ask yourself, "What are the potential outcomes?" and "How likely is this solution to work?" This evaluation step is crucial because it helps you decide on the best course of action. Once you've chosen a solution, it's time to take action! Create a plan for implementing your chosen solution and stick to it.

Let's use Ryan's story to illustrate this. Ryan faced a tough situation during a school project. His team had planned to create a poster for their history class presentation, but they realized their printer was out of ink when the day came to put it all together. Instead of panicking, Ryan suggested they go digital. They could create a slideshow instead! They divided up the work and used the computer lab at school to finish their project. In the end, their creativity not only solved the immediate problem but also impressed their teacher with their unique approach.

It is important to remember that not every solution will work out the first time, and that is completely fine! The process of trial and error is a natural part of problem-solving. Take, for instance, the famous scientist Thomas Edison, who is best known for inventing the light bulb. When he was trying to create a working light bulb, he didn't succeed on his first attempt—or even his hundredth. Edison famously said, *"I have not failed. I've just found 10,000 ways that won't work."*

This attitude of trial and error is key in problem-solving. Each time you try a solution, even if it doesn't work, you're learning something valuable that will help you with the next attempt. Eventually, Thomas's perseverance paid off, leading to significant advancements in electrical technology. So, the next time you encounter a problem, remember that it's okay if your first solution doesn't work out. What's important is to analyze what went wrong and try again. Each attempt brings you one step closer to success.

Do you know how muscles are built when you work out? When you lift weights or engage in physical activities, you're actually causing tiny tears in your muscle fibers. This might sound painful, but it's a crucial part of getting stronger. Your body then repairs these tears, making your muscles bigger and more resilient over time. The same principle applies to developing your problem-solving skills. Each challenge you face is like a workout for your brain. The more you push yourself to think critically and find solutions, the stronger your problem-solving abilities become.

Just like with any workout, consistency is critical. You won't see results overnight, but with regular practice and a willingness to learn from your mistakes, you'll build a solid foundation for tackling future challenges. So, the next time you hit a snag—whether it's in school, sports, or even with your friends—remember that it's all part of the journey. Embrace the challenges and keep pushing yourself. With each problem you solve, you're training your brain and also growing to become a more confident and capable person.

Reflective Question

Take a moment to reflect on your own experiences. What challenges have you faced recently, and how did you solve them?

PRACTICAL EXERCISE 3

1. List at least three responsibilities you have at home or school.

    - ______________________________

      ____

    - ______________________________

      ____

    - ______________________________

      ____

2. Choose one responsibility from your list above. Write a few sentences about how you plan to take ownership of this task to make sure you are always completing it.

    - ______________________________

      ____

    - ______________________________

      ____

- ______________________________

  ____

3. Think about a time you didn't fulfill a responsibility. What happened? How did it affect others?

____

____

____

____

____

4. If you could go back, what would you do differently? How can you make it up to those affected?

____

____

____

____

____

5. Think of a recent problem you faced. Write a brief description of the situation.

____

____

____

____

____

6. Answer the following questions to help clarify the problem:

- What specifically happened?

____

____

____

____

____

____

- Why is this a problem?

____

____

____

____

____

7. Write down at least three possible solutions to the problem you identified. Don't worry about whether they're perfect—just let your ideas flow!

    - ______________________________

      ____

    - ______________________________

      ____

    - ______________________________

      ____

8. Choose one of the solutions you brainstormed. What are the pros and cons of this solution?

Solution:

____

- Pros:

____

____

____

____

____

- Cons:

____

____

____

____

____

9. Write a plan for how you will implement your chosen solution. Include steps you will take and any resources you might need.

____

____

____

____

____

10. How can you apply what you learned from this experience to future challenges?

____

____

____

____

____

“The moment you doubt whether you can fly, you cease forever to be able to do it”

- *J M Barrie, ‘Peter Pan’*

SKILL 4: LEARNING EFFECTIVE COMMUNICATION

In a heated basketball game, your teammate suddenly shouts, "Pass the ball!" You think they want you to pass it immediately, but what they actually meant was to wait until they were in a better position. Suddenly, they get caught off guard and the other team scores. This is exactly how easy misunderstandings can happen, especially when communication breaks down.

Communication goes beyond just talking; it's about making sure your message gets across and that you truly understand others. In this chapter, we'll explore how to become better communicators by focusing on both verbal and non-verbal skills so you can express yourself clearly, listen actively, and boost your confidence in every interaction.

Verbal Communication

Did you know that the average person speaks about 7,000 words a day? That's a lot of chances to communicate! With all that talking, if the person you're speaking to doesn't understand what you’re saying, that’s just equal to you speaking gibberish. That’s why clarity is key in verbal communication.

Verbal communication is about using words to convey your thoughts, feelings, and ideas. It's the most straightforward way to express yourself, but it can also lead to many misunderstandings.

For example, imagine you're at school, and you’re excited to share a funny story about your weekend. If you mumble or speak too softly, your classmates might not catch the punchline, and the moment will fall flat. On the other hand, if you project your voice, you can pull everyone into your story and make them feel like they were there with you.

This doesn't mean you should shout or raise your voice anytime you want to speak, it simply means you are talking loud enough and with the right confidence.

Too quiet = Nobody hears your awesome ideas

Too loud = People might think you're angry

Just right = People want to listen!

Speaking clearly is just the beginning, though. Have you ever noticed how some people can stand up for themselves without making others angry? That's called being assertive.

It is important to be assertive rather than aggressive. Assertiveness means standing up for yourself and expressing your thoughts clearly but respectfully. Aggressiveness means being rude or pushy.

For example, if your friend borrowed your favorite gaming controller and hasn't returned it. Instead of yelling "Why haven't you given me my controller back?" (that's being aggressive) or saying nothing at all (that's being passive), you could try "Hey, I need my controller back for tonight's gaming session. When can you bring it over?" See how that works better? Learning to be assertive helps others understand you without feeling attacked.

Also, when talking to someone, how you say something can be just as important as what you say. When you're excited, let your smile shine through! If you're discussing something serious, make sure your expression reflects the same. Imagine talking about a fun event with a straight face; it can confuse your listeners about how you truly feel. This is where non-verbal communication comes into play.

Challenge For You

Record yourself telling a story and play it back. Sounds weird, right? But it helps you notice if you're mumbling or shouting!

Non-Verbal Communication

Non-verbal communication is all about the messages you send without using words. It includes things like your facial expressions, gestures, posture, and even your eye contact. These cues can say a lot about how you feel and what you mean.

Imagine you're playing a game with friends, and someone scores a point. If you jump up and down with excitement, your body shows how happy you are, even if you don't say a word. But if you cross your arms and frown, it might look like you're upset or frustrated, even if you're just thinking about the next round. Your friends will notice these signals and conclude on how you feel without you having to say anything.

Let's take a look at a situation involving two friends, Sam and Max. One day, Sam was eager to share some exciting news with Max. As he approached Max, he noticed that his friend was sitting at his desk, hunched over with his head down and arms crossed. Sam was buzzing with energy, ready to share his great news, but Max's body language told a different story.

"Hey, Max! I have something awesome to tell you!" Sam said, his excitement bubbling over. But instead of responding with the same enthusiasm, Max looked up slowly and shrugged. Sam paused, recognizing that something was off. Instead of pushing forward with his news, he took a moment to ask, "Are you okay?"

Max's eyes met Sam's, and he opened up about having a tough day and feeling down about a test he didn't do well on. Because Sam noticed Max's non-verbal cues, he was able to support his friend and turn the conversation from being about him to being about Max. This shows how important it is to pay attention to body language and facial expressions.

Now, let's break down some common non-verbal cues/understanding basic body language:

Facial Expressions

Your face can say a lot without using words. A smile can show happiness, while a frown might indicate sadness or confusion. Think about how it feels when you see someone smiling at you; it makes you feel good, right?

Gestures

The way you use your hands can add meaning to your words. If you're excited, you might use hand gestures to emphasize what you're saying. But if you're nervous, you might fidget or keep your hands in your pockets.

Posture

How you stand or sit can send messages, too. Standing tall with your shoulders back shows confidence, while slouching might make you appear less sure of yourself. Good posture not only makes you look more confident but can also help you feel more confident inside!

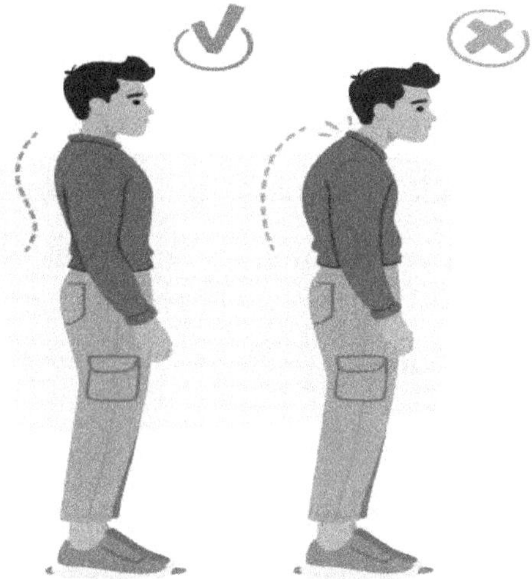

A good and bad posture. Image source: istock

Eye Contact

Making eye contact while someone is talking shows, you're interested in what they're saying. If you avoid eye contact, it might seem like you're bored or hiding something. However, too much eye contact can feel intense, so it's important to find the right balance.

It's also important to be assertive rather than aggressive. Assertiveness means standing up for yourself and expressing your thoughts clearly but in a respectful way. Aggressiveness means being rude or pushy. For example, if you want your friend to stop teasing you, an assertive way to say it would be, "Hey, I don't like that, please stop." An aggressive way might be to yell or say something hurtful back. Learning to be assertive helps others understand you without feeling attacked.

Active Listening

Good communication isn't just about what you say; it's also about how well you listen. Imagine if you were sharing something important and the other person was staring at their phone or looking around. You'd probably feel a bit ignored, right? This is why, when someone is talking to you, you should make sure you are paying full attention and your focus is on their words, not on what you want to say next.

How do you show you are listening actively?

- **Eye contact:** Looking at the person who's talking.
- **Nodding:** Moving your head to show you're following along.
- **Small comments:** Saying things like "I see" or "Uh-huh."

- **Repeating back:** Saying what you heard in your own words.
- **Asking questions:** Getting more information about what they're saying.
- **Giving space:** Letting the other person finish before you talk.
- **Using silence:** Waiting a moment before you respond.

Now, knowing which of these styles to use in your conversation depends on the situation. You don't always have to use all of these methods every time someone talks to you. Different situations call for different tools.

Let's look at a couple of examples:

Your friend Alex is telling you about a movie they saw last night. They're super excited and talking really fast. In this situation:

- Eye contact and nodding would work great. It shows you're paying attention even if Alex is talking too quickly for you to get a word in.

- Small comments like "Wow!" or "Cool!" might work well to show you're engaged.
- Asking questions might not work as well right now because Alex is so excited and wants to share their thoughts without interruption.
- Repeating back what Alex said might slow down their excitement, so it might not be the best tool here.
- Giving space is important - let Alex finish their story before you jump in with your thoughts.

Now, imagine later in the day, Alex seems upset about something but isn't saying much. In this different situation:

- Eye contact is still important to show you care.
- Nodding might only be as useful if Alex is saying a little.
- Small comments might not be enough to encourage Alex to open up.

- Asking gentle questions like "Do you want to talk about it?" might be really helpful.
- Using silence (for a short while) could work well, giving Alex time to gather their thoughts.
- If Alex does start talking, repeating back what you heard could show you're really listening and understanding.
- See how different situations called for different active listening styles? The trick is to pay attention to the person you're talking to and choose the method that fits best.

Solving Problems Without Fighting

Have you ever had a heated argument with your friend about who's better at Minecraft or gotten into a fight with your sibling over whose turn it is on the Xbox? It's easy for things to get out of hand from small arguments. But you could actually solve these problems without all the shouting and fighting.

One of the best ways to handle a disagreement is through what you just finished reading—active listening. Imagine your friend is upset because you keep building huge castles in Minecraft, and they want a turn to lead the building. Instead of arguing back, try listening to how they feel. Say something like, "So, you feel like I always take over, and you want a chance to be in charge too?" When you show you understand their side, they're more likely to listen to you too.

Another key skill is learning how to compromise. Let's say you and your sibling are arguing over who gets the next turn on the Xbox. Instead of letting it turn into a full-blown fight, how about suggesting that each of you gets a shorter playtime so both of you get a turn today? Compromising means neither of you gets exactly what you want, but both of you get enough to be happy. It's all about finding that middle ground.

Other times, the best solution is to come up with a totally new idea that works for everyone. This is called finding a mutually agreeable solution. For example, if you and your friend can't decide whether to play Minecraft or Fortnite, why not take turns every other day? Or better yet, try a completely different game that you both like, so no one feels left out.

To make these conflict-solving ideas work, you need to present them in a way that makes sense to everyone involved. This is where negotiation skills come in. Negotiation is about calmly discussing what you want while being open to what others want too.

If you and your friends are picking a game but you're dying to play soccer and your other friends want basketball, a good negotiation would be suggesting, "How about we play soccer for 30 minutes, then switch to basketball?" Suddenly, everyone wins!

Negotiation isn't about winning or losing. It's about making sure everyone gets something they want.

Specific Communication Scenarios

Remember how we talked in the previous chapter about building positive relationships? Well, good communication is like the secret weapon that helps you do just that!

Communicating with Friends

When you're upset with a friend, your instinct might be to blurt out something like, "You're messing everything up!"

But think about how you would feel if someone said that to you. Instead of blaming, focus on solving the issue together. For example, try saying, "I think we're stuck on this part. How about we figure it out together?" This keeps things positive and shows your friend you value their input.

Another situation might be when a friend feels left out or hurt. Let's say your best friend looks upset after you spend time with someone else. Rather than ignoring their feelings, address it with care: "I didn't mean to make you feel left out. I thought it would be nice to hang out with them, but I'd love to sit with you tomorrow." Acknowledging their feelings shows that you care, strengthening your bond.

The same goes for when it happens to you. Imagine you're in a group project, and your friend seems to be teaming up with someone else more often, leaving you out of important decisions. Instead of stewing in frustration, speak up calmly. You could say, "Hey, I noticed you and Jonny have been making a lot of decisions without me. I feel like I'm not part of the team. Can we work on this together?" This way, you give your friend the chance to understand and adjust.

Sometimes, people don't realize how their behavior might affect others until you point it out. This approach not only helps clear the air but also prevents unnecessary resentment.

Interacting with Family

Let's say you want more time to play video games, but your parents say no because they think it's a distraction. Instead of yelling, "You never let me do anything fun!" try explaining your side calmly. You could say, "I really enjoy playing because it helps me relax after homework. If I finish my assignments early, could I play for an extra 30 minutes?" This is a classic example of good communication with negotiation skills. It shows you're willing to compromise and be responsible, which makes it easier for your parents to consider your request.

Siblings, on the other hand, can be a whole different challenge—especially when it comes to things like deciding who gets to pick the TV show. Instead of grabbing the remote and shouting, "It's my turn!" you can approach the situation with a creative solution that works for both of you.

One idea is to turn it into a short game. For example, you could play rock-paper-scissors to see who gets to watch their show first. This keeps the decision fair and avoids a heated argument. Another option is to agree on a system, like alternating days or splitting the time evenly. Say, "How about you pick today, and I'll pick tomorrow?" or "Let's each watch for 20 minutes, then switch."

Who knows? This playful approach might even make the whole situation fun instead of frustrating.

Engaging with Teachers

Talking to teachers might feel intimidating at times, especially if you don't understand something or need extra help. But why do you have teachers in the first place? To help you succeed, of course. And how can they do that if you don't communicate?

If you're stuck on a math problem or confused about an assignment, don't sit quietly hoping the confusion will magically go away. Raise your hand or approach the teacher after class and say, "I'm having trouble understanding this. Could you explain it in a different way?" This shows you're serious about learning, all teachers appreciate this effort.

Even when you are not struggling, participating in class discussions is a great way to show your teacher you care. For example, if your history teacher asks what you think about a topic, don't be afraid to share your opinion—even if you're unsure it's correct. Saying something like, "I think it might be this, but I'm not 100% sure," shows you're engaged, and it's okay to make mistakes.

Online Communication

A lot of communication happens online today—whether it's gaming chats, texting, or social media. But typing behind a screen doesn't mean words don't have consequences. In fact, what you say online can impact someone just as much as what you say in person. Before you post a comment or share something, ask yourself: "Would I say this to someone's face? Could this hurt someone's feelings?" If the answer is yes, it is better to skip it.

With this mindset, if you ever come across cyberbullying—whether it's happening to you or someone else—don't stay silent. Speak up. Report it. Support the person being targeted. Your action could be the lifeline someone desperately needs. Do what's right without worrying about what others might think. Your courage can make a real difference, and that's all that matters.

In summary, good communication has a sequence:

- Think about what you want to say
- Choose your words carefully
- Watch how the other person reacts,
- Adjust your approach if needed

PRACTICAL EXERCISE 4

1. Write down a short paragraph about a topic you're passionate about. Use clear and exciting language to share your thoughts.

____

____

____

____

____

2. Pair up with a friend or family member. Take turns sharing a story while the other practices active listening. After one person speaks, the listener should:

    - Nod and show engagement.
    - Repeat back what they heard.
    - Ask a follow-up question.

3. Write down one example of a follow-up question you asked:

4. Next time you're in a conversation, pay attention to the other person's body language. Write down what you noticed about their non-verbal cues:

    - Person's Name: ___________________________
    - What did you observe?

5. Imagine you're working on a group project, and your teammate seems frustrated but hasn't said anything. What non-verbal cues might indicate their feelings?

- ______________________________
  ____
- ______________________________
  ____
- ______________________________
  ____
- ______________________________
  ____
- ______________________________
  ____

6. Think about your own communication skills. What is one area you'd like to improve?

____

____

____

7. Write down a specific goal for improving your communication skills this week.

"I have never scored a goal in my life without getting a pass from someone else"

- *Abby Wambach*

SKILL 5: THE SPIRIT OF TEAMWORK AND COLLABORATION

When you think about reaching a big goal, what's the first thing that comes to mind? Do you picture yourself doing it all on your own, working super hard until you finally get it? Let's say you are trying to score a basket in basketball all by yourself while your teammates stand on the sidelines. It's tough, right? But when everyone works together, passing the ball and communicating, you can win the game!

Sometimes, the best way to succeed isn't by doing everything yourself but by working with others to achieve something even better. Whether it's trying to get an A in a tough subject, doing a group project at school, or helping your family at home, teamwork is a skill that can make your life easier and more fun. That's why, in this chapter, we'll explore what teamwork really means and why it's so important to help you become a fantastic team player.

What Is Teamwork?

Josh was excited when his science teacher announced the class would be working on a major project: building a model volcano that would erupt during the presentation. As soon as he heard the assignment, Josh's imagination raced with ideas. He had seen plenty of volcano experiments online, and he was sure he could come up with the best design. In fact, he was already picturing how impressed everyone would be when they saw his volcano erupt in a spectacular burst.

His group was made up of four students: Liam, who was good with art. Ella, who loved details, and Sam, who was always tinkering with things and figuring out how they worked. But Josh wasn't too worried about the others. He already had his own plan and thought if he worked fast enough, he could handle most of the project on his own. After all, how hard could it be?

At the first meeting, Josh came in with his ideas fully formed. He sketched out what the volcano should look like, how it would be built, and even how the eruption would work. He was ready to assign small, easy tasks to his group members while he focused on the important parts. But then something unexpected happened.

Liam didn't like the design. He thought the volcano should look more realistic and wanted to spend time on the art and structure. Ella, who loved details, suggested adding small houses and trees around the volcano to make the scene more complete, but Josh didn't think that was necessary. Sam, on the other hand, wanted to make the eruption even bigger, using different materials to create a more dramatic effect.

Josh started feeling frustrated. No one was listening to his ideas, and the project was quickly turning into something he hadn't planned. The group argued over the next few meetings, with everyone wanting to lead in their way. As time went on, it became clear that they weren't making much progress. The volcano wasn't coming together the way Josh imagined, and the deadline was getting closer.

One night, after a particularly rough meeting where nothing seemed to go right, Josh sat down and looked at the incomplete volcano pieces scattered across his room. He sighed loudly, feeling completely overwhelmed. That's when his mom walked in and noticed the mess—and the look on Josh's face.

"What's wrong, Josh?" she asked, sitting down beside him.

Josh hesitated for a moment but then began explaining everything—how the group couldn't agree on anything, how he had tried to take control of the project, and how no one seemed to be listening to him.

His mom listened patiently, nodding here and there. When he finally finished, she smiled gently and said, "It seems to me like you're treating this like your personal project instead of a group project. Did they choose you as the leader, or did you just take over?"

Josh blinked, caught off guard by the question. "I mean, no one said I was the leader, but I figured since I had the most ideas, I should take charge."

His mom raised an eyebrow. "Hmm, that's interesting. But a group project means working with the whole team, right? It sounds like you've been making decisions on your own instead of letting everyone pitch in. Do you think that might be why they're frustrated?"

Josh thought about it for a moment, and his shoulders slumped. She was right. He had been so focused on making his version of the volcano that he hadn't given his teammates a chance to contribute their ideas. He had been treating the project like it was all about him.

His mom gave him a reassuring pat on the back. "Why not try asking them for their ideas again and really listening this time? You might be surprised at how good the project can be when everyone works together."

Josh smiled, feeling a little lighter. "Thanks, Mom. I think I know what I need to do now."

The next day, Josh called a meeting with his group. This time, instead of telling them what to do, he asked everyone to share their thoughts again. He listened to Liam's ideas for the design, realizing that making the volcano look more realistic would impress their teacher. He asked Ella how she could add details like houses and trees, which would make their project stand out even more. Sam's idea for a more dramatic eruption was risky, but Josh admitted it could make their presentation unforgettable.

Finally, the group started working together. They divided the tasks based on their strengths. Liam focused on the design, Ella worked on the small details, Sam perfected the eruption, and Josh made sure the science behind it all was solid. It wasn't easy; there were still moments when they didn't agree, and there were moments when they got stuck. There was a point when Ella was struggling to figure out how to add the details to the volcano, but now that they were communicating and supporting each other, the rest of the team stepped in to help. Slowly but surely, their volcano began to take shape.

When the day of the presentation arrived, the entire class gathered around to watch their volcano erupt. The volcano looked like a real mountainside, complete with tiny trees and houses around it. Sam's mechanism for the eruption worked perfectly, sending a stream of "lava" flowing down the volcano just as they had planned. Their teacher was blown away, and their classmates clapped in excitement. It was clear that their teamwork had paid off.

As Josh stood there with his group, watching the success of their hard work, he realized something important: without everyone's help and ideas, the project would never have been this good. That's the beauty of teamwork—it's about bringing different talents together and combining them with trust that each person would perform to the best of their abilities to create something better than what any one person could do on their own.

Teamwork is not about one person being the hero. Think of Iron Man. He may seem like a hero who does things on his own, but even Tony Stark didn't really work alone. His suit was powered by the artificial intelligence JARVIS, which constantly helped him in battle, giving him updates, running diagnostics, and keeping him safe. Without JARVIS, Tony wouldn't have been able to handle everything on his own. And when the threats became too big for even him, he brought together the Avengers. Each member of the Avengers had different skills—whether it was strength, magic, or intelligence—and together, they were able to defeat enemies not one of them could have faced alone. That's the power of teamwork.

What Teamwork Is Not

When a team works well together, everyone wins, and the whole group can be proud of what they've accomplished.

But this doesn't mean you always have to agree with everyone or avoid conflict to keep the peace. It also isn't about sitting back and letting others do all the work while you take credit.

Let's break down some common misunderstandings about teamwork:

Teamwork is not avoiding disagreements.

It's okay to have different opinions in a group. In fact, it's usually a good thing! Disagreeing doesn't mean the team is failing; it means people are thinking in different ways, which can lead to better ideas. What matters is how you handle those disagreements—by listening to each other, explaining your points, and finding a middle ground.

Teamwork is not letting one person do everything.

In a good team, everyone contributes. If one person is doing all the work, that's not teamwork; it's unfair. Each member has to take responsibility for their part, and when everyone does their share, the team works more smoothly

.

Teamwork is not just about agreeing with the leader.

Sometimes, people think that being a good team member means always agreeing with whoever is in charge. However, great teams are formed when people bring their own ideas to the table, even if they challenge the leader's opinion. The best leaders listen to their team and know that solid ideas can come from anyone.

Teamwork is not about staying in your comfort zone.

Teams often face challenges, and true teamwork is about stepping up when things get hard. It's about helping each other out when something goes wrong or when someone is struggling. If a problem arises, a good team player doesn't just sit back—they jump in and offer help.

When you keep these things in mind, you'll understand that true teamwork is about cooperation, respect, and shared effort, even when things don't always go smoothly. But when done right, it can lead to amazing results.

The Core Principles of Teamwork

Teamwork can be tough at times, but there are a few key principles that help make it work. When you and your teammates follow these principles, everything becomes easier, and the results are way better. Let's break down these core principles, using Josh's volcano project (and yes, I think we can all agree Josh ended up being the unofficial group leader) as an example:

Communication

Good communication is the backbone of any team. At first, Josh wasn't listening to his teammates, and everyone was talking over each other. However, once Josh started to communicate better, asking for his teammates' ideas and really listening to what they had to say, things began to fall into place. Liam's design ideas, Ella's creative touches, and Sam's engineering skills all came together once they communicated well.

Trust

Trust means believing in your teammates' abilities to get their jobs done in a team. Josh had to learn to trust that Liam could create a great design, that Ella's ideas would make the project stand out, and that Sam's work on the eruption would be safe and impressive. At first, Josh tried to control everything, but once he started trusting his team, everything improved.

Respect

Respecting your teammates' opinions is crucial, even when you don't agree. In Josh's group, everyone had different ideas about how the project should look. Josh didn't agree with some of Liam's or Sam's suggestions at first, but he realized that their ideas brought something special to the project, and they were able to combine the best parts of their ideas.

Respect also means giving credit where it's due. When the volcano turned out great, Josh knew it wasn't just his work—it was a team effort.

Responsibility

Each team member has a role to play, and taking responsibility for your part of the work is important. In Josh's case, he was responsible for making sure the science behind the eruption worked. The rest of the team also had their roles. The project would have suffered if anyone in the group had slacked off or ignored their responsibilities.

But by taking responsibility for their tasks, each teammate helped the project come together smoothly.

Support

Teamwork isn't just about doing your job—it's also about helping each other. Sometimes, a teammate might struggle with a task or feel stuck. That's when stepping in to offer support makes a big difference. For example, when Ella was struggling to figure out how to add the details to the volcano, the rest of the team stepped in to help. This support made the group stronger and more unified.

The Importance of Small Teams and Leadership

One thing that can make teamwork run smoothly even while following the core principles is keeping the team small. Why? Well, when you have too many people, it can be hard to focus and make decisions. Imagine being in a group of twenty people, each with their own ideas about how to do something. It can get messy fast! Too many opinions can slow everything down, and the team might end up arguing all the time instead of working together.

That's why smaller teams are usually better. When you are working with just a few people—maybe five to six—it is easier to hear everyone's ideas and come to a decision. Smaller teams let you share ideas without getting overwhelmed by too many voices.

But even in small teams, it is important to have a leader. A good leader isn't someone who bosses everyone around or ignores what the rest of the team wants. Instead, they help keep everyone on track and make sure things are getting done. They listen to everyone's ideas and help the group figure out which idea to go with.

Sometimes, even with a leader, choosing which idea is best can still be hard. That is when voting comes in handy. Everyone on the team can share their thoughts, and then the group can vote on the idea that works best. This way, everyone gets a say, and the team can make a fair decision.

Once the team picks an idea—whether it is through voting or just discussing it together—everyone has to get behind that decision, even if it wasn't their favorite choice. This is an important part of teamwork: supporting the group's decision and moving forward together.

If you eventually have your team and you discover that amongst you there are teammates who aren't pulling their weight or are causing problems, there are two ways you can go about handling the issue.

Direct Communication

- Talk to the teammate privately
- Explain how their behavior impacts the team
- Use "I" statements like "I feel frustrated when..."
- Be specific about what needs to change

Seek Leadership Support

- If direct communication doesn't work, talk to your teacher or team leader
- Provide specific examples of the problematic behavior for more clarity
- Ask for guidance on resolving the issue

It is also important that you try to look into the underlying issue as to why that particular teammate isn't pulling their weight like they are supposed to. Are they overwhelmed with other responsibilities? Are they unsure of their role or how to contribute? Or maybe they don't feel connected to the rest of the team.

In some cases, the problem might be from a lack of team bonding or clear communication. When team members don't know each other well or haven't had the chance to learn how to work together. That's why team-building games and activities can make a huge difference by promoting collaboration, communication, and problem-solving skills. Here are a few ideas:

The Human Knot

How to Play:

- Everyone stands in a circle, shoulder to shoulder.
- Each person reaches out their right hand and grabs someone else's hand across the circle. Then, they do the same with their left hand, ensuring it's a different person's hand.
- The goal is to untangle the "knot" without letting go of anyone's hands. Teammates must communicate and carefully work together to untwist themselves.

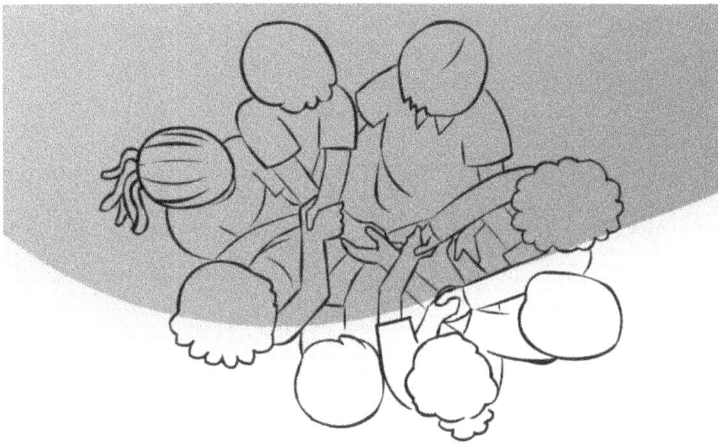

The human knot. Image source: Playmeo

Why It Works: This game teaches patience, teamwork, and clear communication. It forces everyone to listen to each other's ideas and move as a group to succeed.

Escape Room Challenge

What You Need: A space to set up puzzles or a local escape room venue.

If you're setting it up yourself, create a series of puzzles or clues around a room, leading to a final objective (e.g., unlocking a "treasure box"). These could include riddles, hidden keys, or pattern-solving tasks. Divide the team into small groups. Each group works together to solve the puzzles within a set time.

Why It Works: Escape rooms encourage problem-solving under pressure, and success relies on everyone contributing their ideas.

Tower-Building Competition

What You Need: Spaghetti, marshmallows, tape, and string.

How to Play:

- Divide the team into smaller groups (3-5 people).
- Each group gets a limited set of materials (e.g., 20 sticks of spaghetti, 10 marshmallows, and a roll of tape).
- The challenge is to build the tallest tower possible in a set amount of time (e.g., 15-20 minutes).
- At the end of the time, measure each tower and declare a winner.

Why It Works: This game promotes creativity, coordination, and teamwork. It teaches participants to balance competing ideas and make quick decisions as a group.

Blindfold Navigation

What You Need: Blindfolds and an obstacle course (can be simple, like chairs, books, or cones). How to Play:

- Pair up team members. One person is blindfolded while the other acts as their guide.
- The guide must verbally direct their blindfolded partner through the obstacle course without touching them.
- Add challenges like requiring the guide to use specific words or limiting the number of instructions.
- Rotate roles so everyone has a chance to guide and be guided.

Why It Works: This activity builds trust and sharpens communication skills. It also highlights the importance of clear instructions and listening.

Team Trivia

What You Need: Trivia questions related to a specific topic (e.g., a school subject, pop culture, or sports).

How to Play:

- Divide the team into small groups.
- The game leader reads out questions, and teams discuss and write down their answers.
- Award points for each correct answer. Include fun, bonus questions to keep it lively!

Why It Works: Trivia is a great way to mix learning with fun.

Try out any of these activities and you'll find that working in a team becomes easier and more enjoyable.

PRACTICAL EXERCISE 5

Question: What makes YOU a great team player?

____

____

____

____

____

Do you have your answer? If you don't, don't worry! Use this activity to reflect on your past experiences so you have a clear idea of what it takes to be a great team player.

1. Think about a time you worked in a team. This could be a school project, a game, or even helping out at home.

What was your role in the team?

____

____

____

Did the team work well together? Why or why not?

___

___

___

What was the hardest part about working with others?

___

___

___

What was one thing that made the teamwork successful?

___

___

___

2. How well do you listen to your teammates when they share ideas?

3. Do you trust others to do their part, or do you try to control everything?

4. How do you show respect for your teammates' ideas, even when they're different from yours?

5. How do you make sure you follow through on your part of a team project?

6. Do you support a teammate who is struggling with their part of the work? YES/NO

7. Think of a time when someone was the leader of your team (or when you were the leader). What did the leader do well? What could they (or you) improve?

8. Do you believe small teams work better than large ones? YES/NO

9. Next time you work in a team, will you:

- Communicate better? YES/NO
- Build trust with your teammates? YES/NO
- Show respect for everyone's ideas? YES/NO
- Take responsibility for your role? YES/NO
- Support others in the group? YES/NO

Now that you've completed this reflective activity, revisit the question: ***What makes a great team player?***

Based on your answers, write down what you believe makes someone a great team player:

My answer:

____

____

____

____

____

“I can accept failure,

Everyone fails at something.

But I cannot accept ‘Not Trying’

- *Michael Jordan*

SKILL 6: BUILDING EMOTIONAL STRENGTH: EMPATHY, EMOTIONAL INTELLIGENCE, AND RESILIENCE

Sometimes, the strongest people aren't the ones who lift the heaviest weights or win every competition—they're the ones who know how to deal with their feelings. You may not realize it yet, but emotional strength can be just as important as physical strength. It is what helps you understand the people around you and what keeps you going when things don't go as planned. That is why, in this chapter, we are going to explore three of the most important emotional strengths you can have: empathy, emotional intelligence, and resilience.

Emotional Strength 1: Empathy

Empathy is one of those emotional strengths that can make a big difference in how you connect with people. It is what helps you understand how someone else feels, even when they aren't saying it out loud. When you show empathy, you are able to step into someone else's shoes, even if just for a moment, and that helps you respond in a way that makes them feel seen and heard.

Think about a time when a friend seemed upset, maybe after losing a game or having a tough day at school. You probably knew something was wrong, even if they said nothing. You might have noticed they were quieter than usual or saw the look on their face. That's empathy in action—you were able to pick up on their feelings without them having to spell it out for you.

This skill is an important part of building strong friendships and relationships with people around you. Let's say one day during gym class, a classmate gets picked last for a team. They might not say anything, but you can tell by the look on their face that they feel left out. Instead of just ignoring it, empathy would encourage you to reach out by offering them some encouragement. In that moment, you're helping someone feel included when they could easily feel forgotten.

Another example could be when you notice someone sitting alone at lunch. Instead of assuming they want to be by themselves, empathy might nudge you to sit with them or ask if they want to join your group. Sometimes, small acts like this can greatly impact how someone feels, and it all starts with understanding their emotions.

Empathy isn't just something you show when someone is sad or going through a hard time—it also plays a big role when things are going well. Let's say your friend just got some great news, like making the school soccer team. Empathy helps you celebrate with them and share in their happiness because you understand how important that moment is for them. Showing empathy during happy moments strengthens your connection with others, making your friendships deeper.

Now, let's be real: showing empathy isn't always easy. It's not just about recognizing that someone is feeling something—it's about understanding how they feel and why. Sometimes, it's hard to know exactly what someone is going through, especially if you haven't been in their situation. That's why empathy takes practice.

So, how do you practice empathy in your own life? Here are a few simple ways to get started:

Listen Carefully

When someone is talking to you about how they feel, really listen. Instead of jumping in with your thoughts or trying to fix their problem, just listen. Give them the space to share what's on their mind without interrupting. Focus on their words and their feelings. Sometimes, just being a good listener is the best way to show empathy.

Notice Body Language

People don't always tell you how they're feeling in words. Pay attention to their body language—how they stand, what their face looks like, or if they seem different than usual. This can give you clues about their feelings even if they don't say it directly.

Ask Questions

If you're not sure how someone is feeling, it's okay to ask. You might say, "I noticed you've been quiet lately—what's going on?" or "You seem a bit off today. Is everything okay?" Asking gently shows that you care and are open to listening.

Put Yourself in Their Shoes

Imagine how you would feel if you were in their situation. For example, if your friend is really stressed about an upcoming test, think back to a time when you felt nervous about something important. Did you want someone to help, listen, or just be there for you? Thinking about how you would want to be treated can guide how you respond to others.

Offer Help

If a friend or family member is going through something tough, offer to help. Sometimes, just being there or offering to hang out can make a big difference. Even small gestures, like a kind word or a thoughtful message, can show empathy.

If you have been struggling to build meaningful relationships, empathy is the way to go. It goes beyond just being nice. When you show empathy, you help your friends, family, and even people you don't know very well feel understood. You make it easier for others to trust you, and in turn, they're more likely to support you when you need it. It's like a two-way street: the more empathy you give, the more you get back.

Empathy can also help you solve problems. When you take the time to understand how someone else feels, you can avoid misunderstandings and arguments. Let's say you and a friend have different ideas about how to work on a school project. If you use empathy to see things from their perspective, you might find a way to combine both of your ideas or compromise in a way that makes everyone happy.

Empathy doesn't mean you always have to agree with everyone, but it does mean you should try to understand where they're coming from. This is a skill that will help you throughout your life, in school, with your friends, and even as you get older.

Emotional Strength 2: Emotional intelligence

Danny was in the middle of a soccer game when things started to fall apart. His team had been winning for most of the game, but now the other team was catching up. To make things worse, Danny missed a pass that could have scored a goal. He was frustrated, and he could feel his face getting hot with anger. His teammate, Jordan, ran over to him.

"Come on, Danny! What was that?" Jordan snapped, clearly angry too. Danny could feel his anger bubbling up even more. All he wanted to do was yell back and defend himself, but something in him stopped.

Instead of yelling, Danny took a deep breath. He knew that if he let his anger take over, it would only make things worse. He thought about how Jordan must be feeling—probably just as frustrated as he was about the game. Instead of reacting with more anger, Danny said, "I know, man. I messed up. Let's just focus on the next play and finish strong."

Jordan paused for a moment, then nodded. The two of them got back into the game, and while they didn't end up winning, they both played better once they calmed down. After the game, Jordan came over and patted Danny on the back. "Good job keeping it cool out there," he said. Danny's response in this situation is a great example of **emotional intelligence**. But what exactly is emotional intelligence?

Emotional intelligence means being aware of your emotions and knowing how to manage them. It's like having a superpower that helps you recognize what's going on inside you and others, allowing you to react in ways that help, rather than hurt, a situation. Imagine if Danny had yelled back at Jordan. The game would have gone downhill quickly, and their friendship might have been damaged, too. But because Danny was able to stay calm and understand what both he and Jordan were feeling, he helped both of them move past the frustration and focus on the game.

Emotional intelligence is also about being able to "read" the emotions of the people around you. Imagine you walk into a room, and your friend seems really quiet and distant. Instead of assuming they're just being rude or ignoring you, emotional intelligence helps you pick up on the fact that something might be bothering them. You could ask, "Hey, you don't seem like yourself today—everything okay?" That simple question can open up a conversation that helps your friend feel understood and supported.

One of the key parts of being able to read the emotions of others is empathy, which we talked about earlier. It's not just about trying to see if they are alright, it's about knowing how to adjust to their mood and interact with them. Maybe your friend is feeling down because they didn't make the team, and you did, so you avoid bragging about your own success. Or maybe you notice that a classmate is struggling with a lesson, so you offer to help explain it. These small actions show that you're tuned in to the feelings of others, and they can make a big difference.

Emotional intelligence helps you build stronger relationships because it allows you to connect with people on a deeper level. When your friends know that you understand them—not just what they say, but how they feel—they trust you more. They feel like they can come to you with their problems, and they know you'll listen without judgment. Over time, this creates closer and more supportive friendships.

So, how can you practice emotional intelligence? One way is to pay attention to your emotions throughout the day. When you feel angry, frustrated, or stressed, pause for a moment and think about what's causing those feelings. Ask yourself, "How do I want to respond to this? Will my reaction make things better or worse?" By doing this regularly, you'll start to build the habit of managing your emotions healthily.

Another way to practice emotional intelligence is by paying attention to how your emotions affect the people around you. Your mood and actions can have a big impact on others, whether you realize it or not.

For example, imagine you're feeling grumpy one morning because you didn't get enough sleep, and you end up snapping at your sibling for no reason. Maybe they didn't do anything wrong, but because you were in a bad mood, your frustration spilt over onto them. Suddenly, they go from feeling happy and excited to feeling hurt and upset because of your reaction. Emotional intelligence helps you recognize this shift in their mood and understand that your feelings influenced theirs. Once you realize this, it's important to take responsibility for your actions. A simple apology can go a long way in repairing the relationship and showing that you care about how your words or actions affect others.

On the flip side, emotional intelligence also means recognizing when your positive emotions have lifted someone else's spirits. Let's say you're in a good mood one day, feeling upbeat and cheerful. You walk into a room where your friends seem stressed about an upcoming test. You crack a few jokes and encourage them, and soon, everyone starts to relax and even laugh a little. In this case, your positive energy helped change the mood of the entire group. By being aware of this, you can see how your good vibes can spread and make the people around you feel better, too.

Learning to watch how your emotions affect others teaches you two important lessons. First, it helps you understand the power of your actions—whether they're positive or negative. Second, it allows you to make things right when you've unintentionally hurt someone or to boost others when they need a little encouragement.

The more you practice emotional intelligence, the better you'll get at handling tough situations and connecting with others. It's not about being perfect or never feeling upset—it's about understanding your emotions and using them in ways that help you and the people around you.

Emotional Strength 3: Resilience

The rubber band is very unique. You can stretch it, twist it, and pull it in every direction, but no matter how far you stretch it, it snaps right back into shape, ready to be stretched again. In many ways, resilience works the same way. Just like a rubber band, you can face challenges and difficulties, but resilience is what helps you bounce back.

Resilience is the ability to recover when things don't go your way. It is what allows you to keep trying after you've failed, to stay determined when you're disappointed, and to get up again when you've been knocked down.

Life is full of moments where things don't go as planned—whether it's not making the team, not getting the grade you wanted, or something else entirely. Things don't always go perfectly in life, and that's okay. What matters is how you respond when things don't go the way you hoped. This is why resilience is important: it helps you keep moving forward, even when you feel like giving up.

You're preparing for a school play, and you've been practicing your lines for weeks. The day of the performance finally arrives, and when it's your turn to speak, you freeze. Your mind goes blank, and you forget everything you've rehearsed. After the play, you feel embarrassed and upset, but here's where resilience comes in. It teaches you to learn from failure and use those experiences to grow.

When you are resilient, instead of letting that one bad moment keep you down, you remind yourself that everyone makes mistakes. So, you decide to practice even harder for the next performance, and you nail your lines perfectly when it comes around. But even at that, resilience doesn't mean you won't initially feel upset or disappointed when things go wrong. It's normal to feel those emotions. The key is not letting those feelings stop you from trying again. Resilient people allow themselves to feel sad or frustrated, but they don't stay stuck in those feelings. Instead, they figure out how to move past them and get back on track.

For someone who isn't resilient, how do you build resilience?

Developing resilience is like building a muscle—it gets stronger the more you use it. Every time you face a setback and choose to keep going, you are training yourself to be more resilient. It is not always easy, but the more you practice bouncing back, the better you will get at it.

Here are some other ways to build resilience and learn how to bounce back when life gets tough:

Learning from Setbacks

Resilient people don't see failure as the end—they see it as an opportunity to learn. When things don't go your way, ask yourself, "What can I do differently next time?" For example, if you didn't do well on a test, think about how you can change your study habits or ask for extra help. Learning from your mistakes makes you stronger and more prepared for the future.

Staying Positive

Resilience isn't about pretending everything is fine—it is about finding the good even in difficult situations. When something goes wrong, try to focus on what you can control and what is still going well. Maybe you lost a game, but you improved your skills. Perhaps you didn't get the role in the play, but you gained experience. Staying positive helps you stay motivated and keeps you from giving up.

Asking for Help

You may think that being strong means handling everything on your own, but that's not true. Real strength comes from knowing when to ask for help and being open to support from others. Resilient people understand that reaching out to others doesn't make them weak—it makes them smart. Think about it: the best athletes have coaches. The smartest students ask questions in class. Even superheroes team up when the battle gets tough. Iron Man has the Avengers, and Batman has Robin. When you ask for help, you are showing that you're committed to getting better and that you are willing to do whatever it takes to overcome a challenge. Talk to any trusted adult (parents, teachers, friends) when facing challenges and you'll see how much change that would bring.

Why Emotions Matter More Than You Think

Emotions aren't just random feelings that pop up to mess with you. They're actually your body's secret messaging system – intelligent signals that work exactly like the most advanced computer system in the world. When you learn to read these signals, you become unstoppable.

Feeling nervous? That's your "caution" signal

Getting angry? Your "something's not right" alarm

Feeling excited? Your "full power ahead" indicator

Think about NASA's Mission Control. You've probably seen movies about it, like *Apollo 10½: A Space Age Childhood.* Those experts don't panic when unexpected signals come in – they analyze, understand, and respond strategically.

Your emotions work the same way:

- They provide critical information
- They help you make smart decisions
- They protect you from potential dangers
- They guide you through complex situations

If you too, see your emotions this way, it changes things. Your emotions aren't meant to be bottled up (doctors would agree). Instead, think of your emotions as signals to be understood, decoded, and used to become stronger.

How do you do this?

First up is **self-awareness**, and you might remember we talked about it earlier in this guide. Think of it as being a detective of your own feelings. Pay attention to how your body reacts when you're angry, sad, or excited—like your heart racing or your stomach feeling weird. Track patterns in how you react to certain situations and ask yourself, "What's this feeling trying to tell me?" The more you notice, the better you'll understand yourself.

Next is **emotional flexibility**, which is a lot like resilience—we just covered that too. Resilience is your ability to bounce back from tough situations, while emotional flexibility is about being able to bend and adapt without breaking. Think of it like a tree in the wind: it sways and bends, but it doesn't snap. Emotions are the same. No matter how intense they feel, they won't last forever. The key is learning to shift your emotional state. If you're feeling angry or frustrated, try pausing to breathe, watching a funny video, or focusing on something you enjoy. Flexibility is about knowing you can adjust your emotions without letting them control you.

Then there's **emotional expression**. This simply means finding your unique way to let your feelings out. You don't have to shout or keep everything inside. You can talk to someone you trust, like a friend or family member. If talking isn't your thing, try other outlets like drawing, writing, playing music, or even kicking a ball around. The point is to let those emotions out in a way that feels right for you.

Here is a simple method to help you stay cool and in control when emotions run high: **The 4 R Method.**

R1: RECOGNIZE

- Notice the first signs in your body: Tightening stomach, clenched fists, rapid heartbeat, sudden hotness
- Stop and take a breath
- Ask yourself: "What am I feeling right now?"

- Name the emotion specifically: Not just "bad" but "frustrated." Not just "good" but "excited"

R2: REFLECT

- Ask yourself key questions: What triggered this feeling? Where is this emotion coming from? What does this emotion want to tell me?
- Give yourself 30-60 seconds of quiet thought to understand the emotion's message
- Separate the emotion from your actions
- Understand without judging yourself

R3: REFRAME

Transform negative narratives to positive ones (Remember how?)

- From "I can't" to "I'm learning"
- From "I'm a failure" to "I'm learning"
- From "This is impossible" to "This is challenging"

- From "I can't handle this" to "I'm developing skills"

R4: RESPOND

- Take deep breaths
- Count to ten
- Choose actions that make future-you proud

If you are finding it hard to kick into the 4R techniques, here's what you can do

- Stop everything
- Take deep breaths (4-4-4 method: Inhale 4, Hold 4, Exhale 4) Step away from what's making you upset to engage in calming techniques like; Squeezing a stress ball, drawing or doodling, listening to calm music or doing 10 jumping jacks.

Challenge For You

Keep an emotions journal for one month. Note your feelings, triggers, and how you respond.

S/N	CORE EMOTION	Meaning	Alternative Words/Expressions
1.	Sad	Feeling unhappy or low, experiencing emotional pain or disappointment	Bummed, Down, Gloomy, Melancholy, Crushed, Blue, Heartbroken, Miserable, Low-key depressed
2.	Angary	Feeling strong irritation, displeasure, or hostility	Heated, Fuming, Triggered, Annoyed, Pissed, worked up, Frustrated, Steamed, Fired up
3.	Happy	Feeling pleasure, contentment, or joy	Stoked, Pumped, Lit, Thrilled, Buzzed, Psyched, Rad, Awesome, Vibing

4.	Scared	Feeling afraid or frightened	Freaked out, Shook, Anxious, Panicked, wigged out, Terrified, Spooked
5.	Nervous	Feeling anxious or uncertain	On edge, Jittery, Stressed. Wired, Wound up, Antsy, Uneasy, Apprehensive
6.	Excited	Feeling intense enthusiasm or eagerness	Hyped, Amped, Buzzing, Thrilled, Pumped, Stoked, Fired up, Electric
7.	Disappointed	Feeling sad or displeased because	Gutted, Crushed, Bummed, Let down,

		something did not fulfill one's hopes	Wrecked, Blindsided, Deflated
8.	Embarrassed	Feeling awkward or self-conscious	Mortified, Cringing, Awkward, Shook, Humiliated, Dying inside, Uncomfortable
9.	Proud	Feeling deep pleasure or satisfaction from one's own achievements	Stoked, Killing it, Crushing it, Winning, On top, Flexing, Validated
10.	Lonely	Feeling sad from being alone or isolated	Solo, Isolated, Disconnected, Invisible, Abandoned, Left out
11.	Grateful	Feeling appreciative of something received	Blessed, Thankful, Appreciative, Solid, Lucky, Appreciating

12.	Confused	Unable to understand or think clearly	Lost, mixed up, Scrambled, Clouded, Spinning, Disoriented, Baffled
13.	Jealous	Feeling resentful of someone's achievements or advantages	Salty, Triggered, Heated, Pressed, Envious, Bothered, Competition mode
14.	Overwhelmed	Feeling buried under too many emotions or responsibilities	Stressed, maxed out, Swamped, Drowning, Burnt out, Can't even, Overloaded
15.	Confident	Feeling sure of oneself	Solid, Assured, Validated, Powerful, Owning it, Unstoppable, Secure

PRACTICAL EXERCISE 6

Answer these questions to find out which emotional strength you're already great at and which one you might want to work on. Choose the answer that fits you best!

1. When a friend tells you they're upset about something, how do you usually respond?

   a) I listen carefully to what they have to say.

   b) I try to give them advice on how to fix the problem.

   c) I tell them that it is okay to feel bad and that things will get better.

2. If someone is feeling left out, what do you do?

   a) I invite them to join in with what I'm doing.

   b) I ask them if they're okay and see if they want to talk about it.

   c) I think about how I would feel in their shoes and try to help them feel included.

3. When you're feeling frustrated with something, like a difficult homework assignment, what do you do?

a) I try to talk to someone who might help me understand the problem.

b) I stay calm and focus on solving the problem step by step.

c) I keep working on it until I figure it out, even if it takes time.

4. If things don't go your way, how do you handle it?

a) I talk to a friend or family member about how I'm feeling.

b) I take a moment to calm down, then think about what I can do differently next time.

c) I brush it off and remind myself to keep practicing and improving.

5. When you notice someone feeling upset, what's your first thought?

a) I wonder what's bothering them and if I can help.

b) I think about how to make them feel better.

c) I try to imagine how I would feel in that situation.

6. When something feels too difficult or overwhelming, what do you do?

a) I talk to someone who might understand how I feel.

b) I make a plan to break it down into smaller, easier steps.

c) I remind myself that challenges are part of getting better and that I should keep going.

7. If you disagree with a friend, how do you handle it?

a) I try to understand why they feel the way they do.

b) I stay calm and explain my side without getting angry.

c) I let things cool off, then try to fix the situation later.

8. When you face a problem, like a tough project at school, what's your approach?

a) I talk to others to get different ideas on how to tackle it.

b) I stay focused on the task and break it down into smaller steps.

c) I keep going, even if it's frustrating until I find a solution.

9. How do you usually react when someone else achieves something great?

a) I celebrate with them and share in their excitement.

b) I congratulate them but think about how I can learn from their success.

c) I use their achievement to motivate me to work harder on my goals.

10. What do you do when you make a mistake or fail at something?

a) I talk about it with someone I trust and get their advice.

b) I stay calm, figure out what went wrong, and make a plan to do better next time.

c) I keep trying, knowing that mistakes are part of the process.

What Your Answers Say About You

Mostly A's: You are great at empathy! You're really good at understanding how others feel and making them feel supported.

Mostly B's: You are strong in emotional intelligence! You know how to manage your emotions and stay calm in tough situations.

Mostly C's: You are building strong resilience! You don't let setbacks keep you down, and you are always ready to bounce back and try again.

“Digital literacy isn’t just about using technology - it’s about understanding it”

- *Cyber.Civics*

SKILL 7: MASTERING DIGITAL LITERACY

There was a time, not so long ago, when the world felt a whole lot different. Back then, kids spent most of their free time riding bikes, playing outside, and trading stories in person, not online. You would have to actually knock on your friend's door if you wanted to see if they could come out and play. Computers were mostly for school assignments, and mobile phones were just that—phones for calling and texting. There wasn't Instagram, TikTok, or YouTube keeping you glued to a screen all day.

But times have changed. Now, it seems like everyone —from toddlers to grandparents—is online. People are making TikToks before they can even walk, and there's always something new to see on social media. While the internet has made things easier and more fun in many ways, it also means we spend more and more time connected to our screens. And sometimes, it's hard to know when enough is enough. This is why we need to discuss **digital literacy**, which is just a fancy way of saying how well you use technology to find, understand,

and create stuff online. It's like being tech-savvy but with a purpose. It's all about knowing how to navigate the online world, make good choices, and even create your own awesome content. While at it, we'll explore how to be smart about using social media, how to spot dangers online, and how to use technology in a way that works for you—not the other way around.

Understanding social media: How Much is Too Much?

Social media has become a huge part of our lives. It's where you keep up with friends, share cool pictures or videos, and discover the latest trends. Whether it's Instagram, TikTok, or Snapchat, there's always something new to see or do. It's like the world is happening all at once, right on your screen.

And it's not just about connecting with your friends at school. Social media lets you see what's going on with people from all over the world—celebrities, athletes, influencers, and even people who share your hobbies. One minute you are watching a funny meme, the next you're seeing someone break a world record, and then you're back to liking a friend's new post. It's pretty amazing how much is out there.

One of the coolest things about social media is how it gives everyone a voice. Before platforms like YouTube or TikTok existed, you'd need to be a celebrity or have a lot of money to get your ideas in front of a big audience. But now, anyone with a phone and an internet connection can share their thoughts, talents, or creativity with the world. You don't have to be famous to make something that thousands—or even millions—of people see. Whether it's sharing art, music, or just your opinion, social media has levelled the playing field.

Then, there are the challenges and trends. Some are harmless fun, like a new dance routine everyone's trying to learn, while others can even be useful, like workout challenges that get people moving. It feels like there's always something new happening, something you need to check out so you don't miss what everyone's talking about. This can make social media feel really exciting—it keeps you connected to the pulse of what's happening right now. For a lot of people, social media is also where they learn new things. Platforms like YouTube are full of tutorials for almost anything you can think of—whether it's how to fix something, cook, play an instrument, or even study. There are tons of videos and posts out there created by people who love to teach others. In this way, social media has become an amazing tool for learning, where anyone can share knowledge and help others grow.

But like any tool, social media isn't all fun and games. While it's great to stay connected, discover new things, and share your thoughts, there's a side to social media that can sometimes sneak up on you. Without even realizing it, you might find yourself spending more and more time on your phone. What starts out as checking a few new posts turns into hours of scrolling, liking, and watching until suddenly half the day is gone. You might even start to notice that in every free moment you have, you find yourself reaching for your phone due to FOMO (Fear Of Missing Out).

It's not just about the time you spend, though. Social media also has a way of making people feel like they need to be "on" all the time. You see posts of people living what looks like the perfect life—having fun, travelling, winning games, hanging out with friends—and it begins to make you wonder if you're missing out. Everyone is posting their highlights, the best moments of their lives, and that's what you're seeing over and over. But the truth is, nobody's life is perfect, even if it looks like it on social media. People only post the parts they want you to see, and it is easy to forget that there is much more going on behind the scenes than what meets the eye.

Then there's the pressure to keep up. If all your friends are posting, you feel like you should too. If they're getting a lot of likes or followers, you might start wondering why your posts aren't getting as much attention. It can feel like a race to get more followers, more likes, or to be part of the latest trend, and that can become stressful without you even realizing it. Sometimes, it's hard to remember that social media isn't real life—it's just a tiny part of it.

At the same time, it's easy to see why so many people feel pressure to keep up on social media. For some, posting online has become more than just sharing moments—it is actually a job. Influencers, for example, get paid for their posts, and some even receive free products from companies who want them to showcase their stuff. Whether it is promoting clothes, gadgets, or cool destinations, influencers create a steady stream of content to stay relevant and keep their followers engaged.

You might see these creators online and think, "Wow, that seems like the best job ever—getting paid to post about what you like!" And in some ways, it can be. But what most people don't realize is how much work goes on behind the scenes. These influencers spend hours planning, filming, editing, and promoting their content. It's not just about taking a quick photo or video; it often takes multiple tries to get the shot just right, not to mention all the planning that goes into each post. So, while it might look like they're living a dream life, it is actually a lot of work to keep up.

Even if creating content is your goal, endless scrolling and keeping up with everyone else's posts can distract you from achieving it. If you're always watching what everyone else is doing, you're indirectly spending less time working on your own ideas and content. For creators, finding a balance is important because their job depends on their ability to create—not just watch. The more time you spend on other people's content, the less you have for your own.

That is where you need to ask yourself, “How much is too much?”

It also gets tricky here. Why?

Social media is designed to keep you engaged. Have you ever picked up your phone for what you thought was just a quick look, only to realize you’ve been scrolling for an hour? That’s time you could’ve spent learning something new, creating your own videos, or even just relaxing and recharging. There’s always another post, another video, another story. The more you scroll, the more it shows you what it thinks you’ll like, so it’s easy to lose track of time. It’s fun, but it can also become a habit that’s hard to break.

For example, think about when you woke up in the morning. Did you grab your phone before you got out of bed? Did you find yourself scrolling through TikTok or Instagram, watching video after video, until you realized you were late getting ready for school? Or maybe it happened when you got home from school. You meant to check out a few posts, but suddenly it is dinnertime, and you haven’t finished your homework yet. Or maybe you’re studying for a test, and you couldn't resist the urge to check your phone. It is clear that it's becoming addicting.

If you are constantly reaching for your phone during every little break—while waiting for a ride, during commercials, even when you wake up in the middle of the night—it might be a good idea to ask yourself, "Do I really need to be online right now?"

It's not just about losing time, either. Spending too much time on social media can sometimes make you feel anxious or left out, especially if you feel like everyone else is having more fun or doing cooler things. You start comparing yourself to the best moments of other people's lives, forgetting that they have tough days, too—just like you.

So, what can you do if you realize social media is taking up too much of your time?

Set time limits for yourself.

Even influencers, whose job is to be on social media, have to set limits so they don't get sucked into the endless scroll. Without these limits, they wouldn't have enough time to create content that's fresh and exciting. Most phones and apps have settings that let you track how much time you spend on them. You can even set alerts that tell you when you've been on an app for too long. Try setting a daily limit for how long you spend on social media, whether it's 30 minutes, an hour, or whatever feels right for you. Once you hit that limit, log off (resist all temptation and log off) and use your time for something else—whether it's working on a hobby, getting outside, or just relaxing.

Take social media breaks.

Sometimes, the best way to control how much time you spend on social media is to take breaks altogether. Maybe you decide to go a whole day without checking your phone, or you pick one day a week to stay offline. These breaks help you reset and remind you of all the other things you enjoy doing, without the distraction of social media.

Be mindful of how social media makes you feel.

Pay attention to your emotions when you're scrolling. Are you having fun, or is it making you feel anxious, stressed, or left out? If you notice that social media is affecting your mood negatively, it might be time to step away for a bit. Remember, it is okay to log off if something doesn't feel right.

Replace screen time with other activities.

One great way to balance your social media use is to replace some of that screen time with activities that make you feel good. Whether it's reading, drawing, exercising, or hanging out with friends, there are plenty of things you can do that don't involve a screen. These activities not only help you take a break from social media but also give you a chance to relax, have fun, and focus on something that really matters to you.

The key is balance. Social media can be great for connecting, sharing, and learning, but it's important to make sure it doesn't take over everything. When you find yourself spending more time online than with friends in real life, or when you're choosing to scroll instead of doing things you love, it might be time to take a step back. Knowing when enough is enough isn't about cutting out social media entirely—it's about making sure you're using it as a tool that works for you instead of letting it control you.

Digital Awareness And Scams

Not everything you see online is what it seems. In fact, one of the biggest threats on the internet is scams—these are tricks designed to steal your personal information, money, or even your identity. Consider how many ways you interact with technology every day:

- Playing online games
- Searching for homework info
- Watching tutorial videos
- Sharing photos with friends
- Using educational apps

Each of these interactions can be an entry point for scammers.

Scammers can be really clever and tricky—they often disguise themselves as something familiar or even friendly. They might pretend to be a popular game company offering “free points” if you click a link, or they might send a message saying you’ve won a contest you never entered just to get you to give away your email or password.

For example, imagine you get a message from what looks like a well-known game saying, “Congratulations! You have won 10,000 points! Just click here to claim your prize, and a very realistic link will be conveniently placed there.” It sounds exciting, right? But this is a common trick. Once you click on the link, it could lead to a fake website that asks you to enter your password or personal information. The goal of the scammer is to get access to your accounts. They want to use your information for their own benefit, which could lead to a whole mess load of problems for you.

One way to protect yourself is by checking the details carefully. Real companies usually don’t ask for personal information through random messages or emails. Before clicking on any link, ask yourself: *Does this look suspicious? Have I entered any contest to win these points?* If something doesn’t feel right, it is best to ignore the message or ask a trusted adult before taking any further action.

Phishing is another type of online scam that's pretty common. This happens when someone pretends to be a person or a company you know. The scammers use this approach to trick you into giving out personal information. They might send an email that looks like it's from your bank, asking you to "verify your account" by entering your password. But it's not really your bank—it's a scammer trying to trick you.

A good rule of thumb is to never enter personal information into a website or email that you didn't go to on your own or a link which does not start with https//. The 's' in the end of 'http' is to let us know that this website has security protocols in place and is secure.

It's also important to be careful with the information you share on social media. Even simple details, like your birthday or where you go to school, can be used by scammers to guess your passwords or answer security questions. A security question is an extra layer of protection for your online accounts. When you create an account on some platforms that allow two-factor authentication—an additional layer of security asides your password—you'll be asked to choose a special question with an answer that only you would know. For example, "What was your first pet's name?" or "What was the name of your favorite childhood toy?" These questions act like a backup password to help verify your identity if someone tries to access your account.

So, if you post about your favorite pet, a scammer might try using that pet's name to get into your account if they know that's a common security question. This doesn't mean you have to stop sharing things but think twice before posting personal information that others might use to guess your passwords. The key is to choose security question answers that are unique, not easily guessable, and not publicly shared on your social media or other online platforms.

Besides scams, there's also the risk of being tricked by "fake news" or misleading information. Fake news is information that is made to look real, but it is actually false or exaggerated. Sometimes, people create fake news to get attention, sell a product, or even change how people think about something. When you see a surprising story online, it is a good idea to check other sources to make sure it is true. If it is real news, you are likely to find it on several trustworthy websites. But if it's only on one or two unknown sites, it is probably best to ignore it.

Another common scam is a fake website. You might see an ad on social media or a post offering a great deal on something you've been wanting, like a new pair of shoes or the latest gadget, but when you click the link, it takes you to a sketchy website. The website asks for your credit card information, but once you enter it, you never receive the item. Instead, the scammer now has your payment details and can use them to make purchases without your permission.

It's dangerous out there, right? But it shouldn't be if you can be smart. The key to staying safe online is learning how to spot these scams before they get you. So how can you protect yourself from digital scams? Here are some tips:

Be suspicious of emails or messages asking for personal information.

If you get an email or message asking you to click a link or enter your personal details—especially if it's something like your password, credit card number, or Social Security number—be cautious. Legitimate companies usually won't ask for this kind of information through email or text. If you're not sure, don't click the link. Instead, go directly to the company's website by typing the URL into your browser or use their official app to check if there is really a problem.

Look out for signs of phishing.

Phishing emails often have certain clues that give them away. Check the sender's email address closely—scammers will often use an address that is similar to a real one but slightly off (for example, instead of store@company.com, it might be store@compani.com). Also, watch out for spelling mistakes or weird grammar. If the message feels rushed, like it's pressuring you to act fast, it's probably a scam.

Don't trust pop-up ads or deals that seem too good to be true.

If a website offers something that seems way too good to be true, it probably is. Scammers often lure people in with amazing deals that aren't real. Before buying anything from a website you don't know, do some research. Check reviews (the bad ones to be sure) of the site or see if other people have reported it as a scam. Stick to trusted websites and avoid clicking on random ads or pop-ups.

Verify websites before entering personal information.

Before entering any personal information on a website, make sure it is secure. Look for a small padlock icon in the address bar of your browser, and check that the web address starts with "https". As explained earlier the "s" stands for secure. This means the website encrypts your information to keep it safe. If the website doesn't have these security features, it's best to stay away.

Be careful with what you share online.

When you're online, whether you're signing up for a new app, creating a social media account, or chatting with people, think twice before sharing private information. Some details, like your address, school, phone number, or even your full name, should stay private. Anything shared online can potentially be seen by others, even if it is posted in a "private" area. Scammers can use this information to steal from you or even pretend to be you.

It's also a good idea to use strong, unique passwords for your accounts. A strong, unique password should be hard to guess and include a mix of letters, numbers, and symbols. Here's an example:

T! m3toL34rn!2024

Here's why this password is strong:

- It's long – The more characters, the harder it is to crack.
- Uses a mix of characters – It combines uppercase and lowercase letters, numbers, and symbols.
- Not a common phrase – Avoids predictable patterns or common words, making it harder to guess.

Now this might be hard to guess, but if you still want to create a password that you can remember, you can customize it out of your name. For instance, your name is "John." A good password from it can be:

100H#

10: J being the 10th letter of the alphabet

0: Zero in place of the letter O

H: To have a letter in your password

#: In replacement for N

While this is short, it's still a good way to derive a strong password from something you can easily remember.

Another way to create a strong password is to think of a random phrase or sentence you'll remember, then add numbers and symbols. For example, if you love soccer, you could create a password like "Soccer!2023#" instead of just "soccer." Just be sure not to use any personal information, like your name or birthdate, and avoid easy-to-guess words like "password" or "1234."

It's smart not to have the same password for all accounts you might have. This is because if a scammer is able to figure out the password to one account, the rest are at risk too. Try to alternate about 4-5 different passwords among all accounts you might need to create online.

Managing Digital Devices

With so many digital devices around, it is easy to take them for granted. Phones, tablets, and computers are powerful tools that connect you, help you learn, and entertain you, but they also store a lot of important information about you. From schoolwork and personal photos to private messages and passwords, your devices hold pieces of your lives. This makes it important to know how to handle and protect the information on them.

Think about it like this: If you had a box of valuable items, you wouldn't just leave it open for anyone to access. You'd probably keep it somewhere safe and maybe even lock it up. The same idea applies to your digital devices—they're full of things that matter to you, and keeping that information safe is important.

One of the first steps to managing your devices is setting up strong, unique passwords. A strong password is like a lock on the door to your information. Like mentioned earlier, when choosing a password, it is best to avoid easy-to-guess things like "12345" or "password." Instead, pick something that is hard for others to guess but easy for you to remember.

Another important part of managing your devices is keeping your software up to date. This might seem like a small thing, but updates often include security patches that protect your device from new threats. Just like how you'd fix a leaky roof to prevent water damage, updating your device helps protect it from digital "leaks" that hackers could use to break in. Many devices let you set up automatic updates, so you don't even have to think about it.

Let's talk about what happens if you lose your device. Imagine you're at a friend's house and accidentally leave your tablet behind. If it's locked with a password, your information is still safe. But if it is not, someone else could easily access your messages, photos, and other personal data. That is why setting up a password or a PIN is crucial—it is a simple step that adds a lot of security.

Backing up your information is another essential part of managing your devices. Backups are like copies of everything important on your device, stored either on the cloud (online) or on a physical device like a USB drive. Backing up your information means that if anything ever happens to your device—like it gets lost or breaks—you won't lose your photos, homework, or other important files. Many devices have settings that allow you to automatically back up your data regularly, so you don't even have to remember to do it.

IMPORTANT: When it comes to backing up your data, the password for your backup is crucial. This password needs to be your strongest and most complete and should not be used as the password to any other accounts you have. Think of your backup password as a super-secure vault. If someone gets into this, they could access ALL your personal information. So, make it as tough to crack as possible. Treat this password like the ultimate guardian of your digital life.

Staying organized on your devices can also help. With so many apps, files, and photos, things can get cluttered fast. Just like you wouldn't let your room get so messy that you can't find your stuff, keeping your digital space tidy is a good idea. Organize your apps into folders, delete files you don't need, and use a storage plan to manage your photos and videos. This will make it easier to find what you need when you need it.

It's also a good idea to log out of accounts when you're finished using them, especially on shared devices. If you're using a school computer or a friend's phone, make sure to log out of your email, social media, or any other account before you leave. But don't stop there—clear the browsing history or any saved login details to make sure your information isn't stored on the device. Logging out and clearing your tracks helps protect your information from being accessed by anyone else after you're gone.

Managing digital devices also means being aware of the risks that come with downloading files and apps. It can be tempting to download cool new games or fun tools, but not every app or file is safe. Some downloads contain viruses—harmful software that can damage your device or steal your information. Before downloading anything, make sure it's from a trusted source, like the official app store or a website you know is safe. Reading reviews and checking ratings can also tell you if the download is safe.

At the end of the day, managing your digital devices is about treating them with care and responsibility.

Essential Digital Skills for Young Creators

Having good digital skills can make your life easier. Whether you're working on a school project, sending an email, or sharing content online, having these skills will definitely help you stand out.

Creating Digital Content

Digital content is anything you create and share using technology. It could be a class presentation, a TikTok video, or even a simple animation.

Presentations

Presentations are a fantastic way to share ideas, explain a topic, or showcase your work. For example, you might use them for a school project to visually present your research or for a creative assignment.

Programs like Google Slides, PowerPoint or Canva make it easy to create professional-looking slides. Learn to use these tools to add colorful images and simple animation.

When making your slides, keep them clean and not too crowded. Follow the templates provided and choose fun but readable fonts.

Video Creation

Want to make a TikTok, a short YouTube video, or a quick animation for fun or school? Videos are a powerful way to tell a story or explain something.

Tools to Try:

- **TikTok:** Perfect for creating fun, short videos with music and effects.
- **iMovie:** Great for editing videos on Apple devices.

- **CapCut:** A user-friendly video editor perfect for TikToks or short videos on both IOS and Android devices.
- **InShot:** Great for editing videos and photos and compatible with both IOS and Android devices.
- **Canva:** Also offers tools for creating short animations. Compatible with both IOS and Android devices.
- **Scratch:** Beginner-friendly site for creating simple animations.

You can start with short, 12-minute videos to learn basic editing: trimming clips, adding music, using transitions and adding simple text overlays or captions.

Email Etiquette

Email might feel a little formal compared to texting, but it's an important skill to master for school and beyond. Knowing how to write a proper email shows respect and professionalism.

Tips for Writing an Email:

1. **Subject Line**: Be clear and specific. Instead of "Help," write "Question About Homework Due Friday."

2. **Greeting**: Always start with a polite greet, such as "Dear Mr. Smith" or ", Hi Ms. Jones."

3. **Body**: Keep it short and to the point. Explain why you're writing and what you need.

4. **Closing**: End with a polite sign-off, like "Thank you," or "Best regards," followed by your name.

Example Email:

Subject: Request for Extra Help on Math Assignment

Dear Mr. Johnson,

I hope you're doing well. I'm having some trouble understanding question 5 on the math assignment and was wondering if you could explain it in class tomorrow.

Thank you for your time!

Best regards,

[Your Name]

Digital Citizenship

Being a good digital citizen means using the internet responsibly, safely, and respectfully. The internet is a big part of our lives—it's where we learn, play, and connect with others. But just like in the real world, there are rules to follow and risks to watch out for.

First, let's talk about respecting other people's work. When you're online, you might find cool images, videos, or music that you'd love to use for a project or post. But just because it's online doesn't mean it's free to take. This is where copyright comes in. Copyright laws protect creators and their work, just like you'd want someone to respect your creations. If you need content, use resources like Unsplash or Pixabay that offer free and copyright-safe options. Respecting copyright is more than following the law—it shows integrity and fairness, qualities that every good digital citizen should have.

Another important part of being a digital citizen is staying safe when interacting with others online. The internet allows you to talk to people from all over the world, but not everyone you meet online is who they say they are.

This is called "stranger danger," and it is something to be cautious about. Strangers online might pretend to be someone your age or share your interests to earn your trust. They might ask for personal information like your name, address, school, or phone number. Never share these details with someone you don't know in real life. If a stranger messages you, it's okay to ignore them, block them, and let a trusted adult know. Your safety always comes first.

Finally, let's address cyberbullying—a major issue that can hurt people deeply. Cyberbullying happens when someone uses the internet to send mean messages, spread rumors, or embarrass someone else. This can happen on social media, in games, or even through text messages. If you ever face cyberbullying, don't respond to the messages—that's what the bully wants. Instead, save screenshots as evidence, block the bully, and report their behavior to the platform. Most platforms, like TikTok and YouTube, have tools to help you do this. Make sure to talk to a parent, teacher, or trusted adult who can support you. If you also see someone else being bullied online, don't stay silent. Stand up for the person by reporting the bully and offering support to the victim.

Resources you can use for handling include:

- **Stop Non-Consensual Intimate Image Abuse:** Helps remove and prevent the sharing of intimate images without consent.
- **Stay Safe Online:** Provides tips and resources for safe internet use.
- **Cyber Civil Rights Initiative:** Offers help for victims of online harassment.
- **Online Safety by Feminist Frequency:** Guides on staying safe online.
- **StopCyberBullying.org:** Programs to help address cyberbullying.
- **FBI Internet Crime Complaint Center (IC3):** A place to report suspected internet crimes.

Report bullying.

Being a good digital citizen isn't just about keeping yourself safe—it's about contributing to a respectful, positive, and safe online community. Remember: your actions online matter, and you have the power to make a difference.

Solving Problems Through Online Research

The internet is like a giant library with endless shelves, full of information on almost anything you could imagine. It's become one of the best places to find answers, learn new things, and solve problems. Whether you're looking for help with homework, trying to understand a new hobby, or just curious about a topic, online research can be incredibly useful—as long as you know how to do it wisely.

When you are faced with a question, the first step is usually to go to a search engine like Google. You type in a few words, hit enter, and instantly get thousands—sometimes millions—of results. But with so much information available, how do you know what to trust? That's where learning smart online research skills comes in.

Start by thinking about the words you type into the search bar. These words are called “keywords,” and they help narrow down the search results to the most relevant information. For example, if you’re working on a science project about the solar system, typing “solar system facts for kids” might give you results that are easy to understand. But if you type “solar system,” you might get more complex articles intended for adults. By choosing your keywords carefully, you can find information that fits what you need.

Another helpful trick is to use **search operators**—special symbols and characters that help you get more specific results. Here are a few that will make your searches much more efficient:

- **Quotation Marks (“”)**: Use quotation marks around phrases or specific terms to get results that include exactly what you’re searching for.
    - Example: Searching for **"I love you Mom"** will return results with that exact phrase.

- **Dashes (-)**: If you want to exclude a certain word from your search, place a dash (-) in front of it.
    - Example: Searching for **dolphins -football** will exclude results related to football, showing only dolphins-related content.
- **Tilde (~)**: Use a tilde (~) in front of a word to include results with synonyms of that word.
    - Example: Searching for **music ~classes** will return results including related terms like lessons or coaching.
- **Site Search (site:)**: Use **site**: followed by a website URL to search within that specific website.
    - Example: Searching for **site:ndtv.com** will give results from only the NDTV website.
- **Vertical Bar (|)**: Use a vertical bar (|) to search for results that contain any of the terms separated by the bar.

- Example: Searching for **blouse | shirt | chemise** will show results with any of those terms.

- **Two Periods (..) for Range**: Use two periods (..) between numbers to search within a range.
  - Example: Searching for **movies 1950..1970** will return results about movies released between 1950 and 1970.

These tricks can save you time and make your searches much more accurate. By knowing how to filter out unnecessary results and focus on exactly what you're looking for, you can find the answers you need faster and more efficiently.

Once you have your search results, it is important to evaluate the sources. Not everything you read online is true or reliable, so it is good to check who wrote the information. Trusted sources often include websites that end in .edu (educational institutions), .gov (government websites), or well-known organizations. Websites for popular magazines, news outlets, and science organizations can also be reliable, but it's always a good idea to check a few sources to confirm what you find.

It's also helpful to check the date of the information. Some topics change over time as new research is done or new discoveries are made. If you're researching technology or science, for example, articles that are a few years old might be out of date. Try to look for information that has been published recently so you're getting the most current facts.

When doing research, be careful about websites that make extreme claims or ask you to "click here" for amazing offers. These can sometimes be scams or sources of misinformation. A good rule of thumb is that if something sounds too good to be true, it probably is. Reliable information is usually straightforward and backed up by facts or studies, not exaggerated promises.

Another smart way to improve your research skills is by learning to use different types of sources. Besides search engines, there are online encyclopedia like Wikipedia, video platforms like YouTube, and even online databases filled with academic articles. Wikipedia can be a great starting point for basic information, but keep in mind that anyone can edit it, so it's not always accurate. It's best to use Wikipedia as a starting point and then find more reliable sources to confirm the information.

Sometimes, video tutorials can be helpful too, especially if you're trying to learn a skill like playing an instrument, coding, or fixing something around the house. Many creators on platforms like YouTube make high-quality educational content, but it is essential to consider the creator's credibility, as with written sources. For example, a science experiment video from a science channel is likely more trustworthy than a random video with no explanation.

Here's a tip for organizing information as you find it: create a list or document with the most important points from each source. This way, you won't have to go back and find each website later. You can jot down the key facts, take notes, or even copy links to revisit if you need more details. Organizing your research this way can help make projects easier, especially if you're working with a lot of information.

Another part of smart research is knowing when to stop. Sometimes, researching can turn into endless searching, with one link leading to another, and before you know it, you're reading about something totally different from where you started! If you feel like you've found good, solid answers, it's okay to stop and move forward with what you've learned.

In the digital age, knowing how to find and use information wisely is one of the most valuable habits you can develop. With these pro search techniques, you'll be ready to tackle any topic, whether it is for a school project, a new hobby, or just something you're curious about. Just like any skill, the more you practice, the better you'll get.

PRACTICAL EXERCISE 8

Task 1

Choose a topic you're curious about (e.g., endangered animals, space exploration). Find 3 different websites with credible information

Write down:

Website name

____

____

Why you think it's trustworthy

____

____

____

One interesting fact you learned

____

____

____

Task 2

Create a 5-Slide Presentation using PowerPoint

Theme Options (Choose One):

- My Future Career
- My Favorite Hobby
- An Important Global Issue
- A Place I Want to Visit

Slide Requirements:

Slide 1: Title slide with creative design

Slides 2-4: Content with images

Slide 5: Conclusion/Summary

Scoring Checklist:

- Clear message
- Visually appealing
- Correct information
- Interesting design

Task 3

Design a Motivational/Informative Poster with Canva

Choose a Topic:

- Mental Health Awareness
- Environmental Protection
- Anti-Bullying
- Staying Healthy
- Following Your Dreams

Design Requirements:

- Use at least 3 colors
- Include a catchy headline
- Add 1-2 relevant images
- Make text readable
- Include a call to action (where to sign up, how to contact, media pages to follow etc.)

Scoring Checklist:

- Clear message
- Visually appealing
- Creative layout
- Emotional impact

Task 4

Write an email to:

- A teacher

- A family member
- A potential mentor

Email Purpose Options:

- Ask about a program
- Share an interesting observation
- Request information
- Express appreciation

Scoring Checklist:

- Clear subject line
- Proper greeting
- Concise message
- Polite closing
- Proofread

SKILL ACHIEVEMENT LEVELS

0-1 Completed: Digital Beginner

2 Completed: Digital Explorer

3 Completed: Digital Master

4 Completed: Digital Superhero!

Find a parent/guardian/friend/sibling to validate your projects and sign below.

Signature: ____________________

Date: ________________________

"Before you can become a Millionaire - you must learn to think like one"

- *Thomas J Stanley*

SKILL 8: FINANCIAL LITERACY

Imagine you're holding a crisp $20 bill in your hand. That single piece of paper could become your favorite new video game, five ice cream sundaes, or even grow into something bigger—like that awesome bike you've been eyeing. But here's the thing: money has different possibilities depending on how you use it. This is something no school or college will ever teach you.

When you understand how money works, it's like unlocking special powers to make it go further. You could spend it all at once, save it up for something big, or even invest it to make it grow over time. Each choice brings a different result, and that's what financial literacy is all about—learning how to make smart choices with your money.

This chapter will tune your mindset towards money in a whole new way—as a tool you can shape to fit your dreams, needs, and plans. You'll learn the basics of budgeting, saving, and even investing so that the $20 bill—and all the money you handle—works harder and smarter for you.

Know The Value Of Money

Have you ever wondered why your parents say, "Money doesn't grow on trees"? You've probably heard it a hundred times. Maybe you asked for a new video game or those trendy sneakers everyone's wearing, and your parents sighed and said those familiar words. You might be thinking, "I know it doesn't—that's why I'm coming to you for it!"

You've got a point! You're doing exactly what makes sense: asking instead of expecting money to magically appear. But here's the thing—your parents aren't trying to give you a lesson in botany. They're actually sharing something much more important about what money really is.

Think about your parents' wallet or purse as their own special kind of tree. Instead of growing money with water and sunlight, this "tree" needs their time, energy, and hard work. Every morning, when they head off to work, they're "watering" that money tree with hours of effort, which then "grows" enough to cover groceries, gas, school supplies, and maybe—just maybe—those new sneakers you're hoping for.

But unlike real trees, which can grow new leaves pretty quickly, your parents' money tree has limits. They have to decide carefully which "leaves" to pick and when. Should they use it for sneakers now, or save it for next month's soccer registration? Should they get that video game you want, or put it aside for an upcoming family trip? Since money doesn't magically refill itself, they have to be mindful of how they divide it. Think of their earnings as water in a bucket—they have to choose how much goes toward housing, food, savings, and yes, sometimes those sneakers you've been eyeing.

Now, let me make this real for you. Suppose you're saving up for a $60 video game. If you got a job where you earn $10 an hour, you'd need to work six whole hours to buy it. That's nearly an entire school day—plus an extra hour—just to earn enough for that one game. Seeing it this way helps you understand why making thoughtful choices about money is important. This doesn't mean you can't buy things you want. It just means that thinking about your choices is part of respecting the effort that goes into earning money. When you save up for something special, hunt for the best deals, or wait for a sale, you're showing that you understand the value of money—and how hard people work to earn it.

But here's something interesting to think about: why do we even need money in the first place? Long ago, people didn't have dollars or coins. Instead, they traded things directly – like swapping a chicken for some vegetables or trading handmade clothes for tools. It sounds simple, but imagine trying to buy a video game with chickens! Sounds silly and unfair right?

Money makes trading much easier. Think about trying to sell your old bike. Without money, you'd need to find someone who not only wants your bike but also has something you want in return. That's not just inconvenient – it would take a lot of time and effort to find that perfect match! With money, you can sell your bike to anyone interested and then use that money to buy what you need from someone else. Money basically acts as a middleman, allowing you to trade your time and effort (or things you own) for other things, even if the people you're trading with don't want exactly what you have.

But beyond making things more convenient, money has an even greater value. Think about that new iPhone you've been eyeing or the game console you'd love to have. It's one thing to want it, but without money, that want is just a wish. You can't just walk into an apple store and pick up an iPhone without payment. This is where money shows its real value.

It's not just about numbers – it's about freedom and choice. Money is what turns your wishes and goals into things you can actually achieve. Whether it's something small, like a snack after school, or something big, like a car one day, money is the tool that lets you reach for those things. With money, you're able to get the things you need, like food or school supplies, and the things you want, like a new gadget or concert tickets. Without it, those things stay out of reach.

Money Around the World

Money isn't the same everywhere. Different countries have different types of money called currencies. Think of it like this: each country has its own special kind of money. In the United States, we use dollars. But if you go to Japan, they use yen. And if you visit Mexico, they use pesos. Some countries in Europe even share the same currency called the euro.

When you travel to another country, you might need to exchange your money for their currency. This is called foreign exchange. It’s like trading in-game currencies between different video games. Just like you can't use V-bucks from Fortnite to buy stuff in Roblox, you can't use American dollars to buy a burger in Japan.

You can easily exchange money at banks, special stores, or even at the airport. They will tell you how much of your money is equal to their money. This is called the exchange rate. Foreign exchange isn't just for travelers. It's also super important for businesses that buy and sell things between countries. For example, if a company in the United States wants to buy toys from a company in China, they need to pay in Chinese yuan. So, they will exchange their dollars for yuan to make the purchase. The same thing happens when other countries want to buy things from the United States. They need to exchange their currency for dollars. Foreign exchange helps businesses all over the world trade with each other and keep the global economy moving!

Country	Currency	Symbols
United States	United States Dollar (USD)	$
Eurozone	Euro (EUR)	€
United Kingdom	British Pound Sterling (GBP)	£
Japan	Japanese Yen (JPY)	¥
Canada	Canadian Dollar (CAD)	CA$
Australia	Australian Dollar (AUD)	AU$
India	Indian Rupee (INR)	₹
China	Chinese Yuan Renminbi (CNY)	¥

Switzerland	Swiss Franc (CHF)	CHF
Brazil	Brazilian Real (BRL)	R$
South Africa	South African Rand (ZAR)	R
Russia	Russian Ruble (RUB)	₽
Mexico	Mexican Peso (MXN)	MEX$
Singapore	Singapore Dollar (SGD)	S$
Turkey	Turkish Lira (TRY)	₺
South Korea	South Korean Won (KRW)	₩
New Zealand	New Zealand Dollar (NZD)	NZ$

Thailand	Thai Baht (THB)	฿
Indonesia	Indonesian Rupiah (IDR)	Rp
Nigeria	Nigerian Naira (NGN)	₦

Note: Some currencies share the same symbol; for example, the dollar sign ($) is used by multiple currencies, including the United States Dollar and the Mexican Peso. To avoid confusion, prefixes like 'CA$' (Canadian dollar) are used.

Different Forms of Money

Money itself comes in various forms, each offering unique ways to manage and spend your finances.

Cash

Cash refers to physical currency, such as coins and paper bills. It's the most direct way to pay for goods and services. While universally accepted, carrying large amounts can be risky due to potential loss or theft. It's also very difficult to track cash spending.

Checks

Checks are like written promises to pay. When you write a check, you're telling your bank to pay a specific person or organization a set amount of money. They're less common now but still used, especially for larger payments. However, they require time to process and clear.

Debit Cards

A debit card is linked directly to a bank account. When you use it to make a purchase, the money is deducted immediately from the account. If you have $50 in your account, you can only spend $50. This helps prevent overspending and teaches you to manage money responsibly. Additionally, debit cards can be used at ATMs to withdraw cash, and every transaction can be tracked.

Credit Cards

Credit cards are more complex. When you use a credit card, you're actually borrowing money from a bank with a promise to pay it back later. But it comes with important responsibilities. Every time you use a credit card, you are creating a debt that must be repaid, often with extra charges called interest if not paid in full by the due date. This means if you buy something for $100, you might end up paying $110 or more if you don't pay it back quickly.

The Power of Saving and Investing

So, let's go back to that $20 bill we talked about earlier. It could buy you a few fun things right now—a game, some snacks, or maybe even some small accessories. But what if, instead of spending it all at once, you made that $20 work for you over time? That's where saving and investing come in, two of the most powerful habits you can develop. They might sound simple, but when you understand how they work, they can help you do a lot more with your money—and they can change the way you think about what money can do for you.

Saving

I'm pretty sure I don't need to explain what saving is. Your parents have probably mentioned it once or twice (or a hundred times). They might have also given you a piggy bank (one you occasionally shake to see if it feels heavier) to "encourage" your savings. yes?

Well, if it's not this, you've probably at a point saved on your own. Like that time, you put aside some of your allowance to buy a secret gift for someone you like, where asking your parents for extra money wasn't exactly an option.

But saving isn't just about putting away money; it is not only when you have a goal in mind, like buying a gift for your favorite person. It is about creating a habit—a routine that becomes second nature and has the power to give you something more: freedom. Freedom not just for what you know you want right now but also for the things you might want down the road, even the ones you can't imagine yet. That's why saving works best when it's regular: putting aside a specific amount of money on set days or weeks. This way, you're truly cultivating the habit of saving, setting yourself up for a future where you are prepared for anything.

Think of it like creating a treasure chest just for you. Every time you add to it, that treasure chest fills up a little more.

Let's imagine this in action. Say you're 12 years old now, and you decide to save $5 every week. You make it a routine, setting aside that $5 no matter what, just like a regular chore. If you keep doing this until you turn 18, let's see how much you'd have saved.

If you save $5 each week, that adds up to $260 in a year. Over six years, from ages 12 to 18, that totals $1,560. That's a solid amount accumulated from consistent, small contributions. By 18, you wouldn't just have a treasure chest; you'd have built yourself a solid foundation. And with that, you'd be in a position to start something even bigger—like an investment plan. That's how saving now can set you up for amazing opportunities later.

Tips on How to Start Saving

Whether you're getting an allowance, doing extra chores, or earning a bit from a summer job, here's how to start building smart saving habits that don't require a lot of money:

Set a Small, Fun Goal

As a beginner, you might find saving to be much easier when you have a goal in mind. Start with something simple—maybe a book, a new game, or a fun outing with friends. Write down how much it costs, and then figure out how much you need to save each week to reach that amount. For example, if your goal is to save $20, putting aside just $2 or $3 a week will get you there in a couple of months.

Save a Little Each Time You Get Money

Whenever you receive money—whether it's from an allowance, birthday gifts, or small jobs—get into the habit of saving a part of it. A good rule to follow is to save at least 10-20% of whatever you receive. So, if you get $10, try to put $1 to $2 in savings right away. It may not seem like much, but over time, these small amounts will grow. Also, having this balance helps you enjoy spending while still working toward something bigger.

Create a Savings Jar or Envelope

Seeing your savings grow can be motivating. Set up a jar, envelope, or even a small box labelled with your goal. Each time you save money, add it to your "savings jar". If you're using a jar, give it a little shake to hear the coins clink or feel the weight of the envelope increase as you add more bills. This sound or weight will remind you of your progress, giving you a sense of accomplishment and keeping you excited about reaching your goal.

Challenge Yourself to Save a Little Extra

If you have a week where you get a little extra cash, try saving more than usual. For instance, if you normally save $2 a week, aim to save $3 or $4 just for that week. It might not sound like a big difference, but every extra bit brings you closer to your goal faster.

Keep Track of Your Progress

Tracking your progress can be fun and helps you stay focused. Create a small chart or use a notebook to record each amount you save. Mark your goal at the top and update it every time you add to your savings. You'll feel more encouraged to keep going when you see how much closer you're getting each week to your goal.

Savings Tracker Chart

Savings Goal: [Write Your Goal Here]

Goal Amount: [Write the Total You Need to Save]

Date	Amount Saved	Total saved so far	Notes/Motivation
MM/DD /YYYY	[Amount]	[Total]	Keep it up!
MM/DD /YYYY	[Amount]	[Total]	Great job saving!
MM/DD /YYYY	[Amount]	[Total]	Almost halfway there!
MM/DD /YYYY	[Amount]	[Total]	Final stretch—almost there

Total Savings Goal: ____________________

Final Total Saved: ____________________

❖ Investing

Now, let's talk about investing. Once you're comfortable with saving, investing is the next step that can really amplify the power of your money. Investing means putting your money into something that has the potential to grow over time. Think of it like planting a tree—you're putting your money into the ground and letting it grow into something bigger.

It's easy to think about investing as something only grown-ups do, but it's not. You can start investing in small ways, like putting your money into an account that gives you interest. Interest is money the bank pays you just to keep your money with them. It's like a reward for not spending it immediately.

Imagine after saving that $260 for the first year, you decide to put the money in a bank account that gives you 5% interest. After a year, that $260 will grow by $13, bringing your balance to $273. Now, $13 might not seem like a huge amount, but here's the exciting part: as your balance grows, so does the amount of interest you earn. It's like a snowball effect—the more you save and invest, the bigger your "snowball" of money becomes.

This is called the "compounding effect," which means that the more you save and invest, the faster your money builds on itself. In the second year, you'd earn interest not just on the original $260, but on the entire $273, giving you a little extra. Over several years, this compounding effect makes a big difference, helping your money grow faster than it would from saving alone. It's one of the best ways to make your hard-earned savings work even harder for you.

Your part is to understand that investing is not about quick wins or instant results. It's about planting seeds now and allowing them to grow in the future. Over time, small investments can grow into big ones, giving you the financial freedom to pursue your goals without always having to rely on your parents, a paycheck or asking for more money.

That's why it's important to start early. The earlier you start saving and investing, the more time your money has to grow. Just like a plant needs time to become a tree, your money needs time to grow and multiply.

Types of Investments to Start With

When it comes to investing, there are several beginner-friendly options that don't require a lot of money or experience. Here are a few examples:

Savings Accounts with Interest

A bank account is a secure place to store your money instead of keeping it in cash, which could easily get lost. The bank keeps your money safe, and in return, you get access to an account that you can manage with the help of your bank's services. A savings account is one of the simplest ways to start investing. When you put your money into a savings account at a bank, the bank thanks you by paying a little extra money, called interest, just for keeping your money there. It's like a reward for not spending all your money right away. Over time, the interest adds up, helping your money grow bit by bit.

Certificates of Deposit (CDs)

A Certificate of Deposit, or CD, is like a savings account but with a twist. When you open a CD, you agree to leave your money in the bank for a certain period—maybe six months or a year. In exchange, the bank pays you a higher interest rate than a regular savings account, so you'll earn a bit more. The only rule is that you can't touch the money until the time is up, which makes it a great option for money you don't need to spend any time soon.

Bonds (or "Lending Money")

A bond is like lending your money to someone else for a set period. Usually, people buy bonds from the government or big companies, but here's an idea to help you understand how bonds work: Imagine you're older sibling wants to buy something but doesn't have enough cash, so they ask you to lend them $10. You both agree that in a few weeks, they'll pay you back, plus an extra $1 to thank you for lending them the money. That extra $1 is like interest on a bond!

Stocks (or "Buying a Small Part of a Business")

Stocks are pieces of a company that people can buy. When you buy a stock, it's like owning a small part of that business. If the company does well and grows in value, your stock becomes worth more, meaning your investment grows too. Stocks can be a bit more unpredictable, as companies can go up or down in value, but they also offer the potential for bigger rewards.

If you're interested in trying out some of these ideas, start by having a conversation with your parents or a trusted guardian. Explain that you'd like to learn about investing and see if they're open to helping you practice with small amounts. You might start by opening a savings account to earn a little interest, or you could try lending a small amount to a family member as a "bond" and agree on a repayment with interest. Make sure you have a written document about any agreements with both parties' signatures.

This way, you can safely learn the basics of investing in a way that's both fun and practical. Starting small and learning step-by-step will give you a solid foundation for making smart money choices in the future.

Saving vs. Investing: When to Do Each

Both saving and investing are useful, but they're suited to different goals. If you want to buy something soon, like in a few months, saving is your best option because it's safer and easily accessible. But if you're planning for something further in the future, like a college fund or a future car, investing could be a better choice, as it allows your money to grow over time.

Ultimately, both saving and investing give you something valuable: the power of choice. With these tools, you're in control of what to do with your money now and in the future. Maybe you'll choose to treat yourself to something special after reaching a savings goal, or perhaps you'll let your investments grow, building a nest egg for future opportunities. Either way, the more you practice saving and investing, the more natural it becomes.

One day, when you're older and facing bigger financial decisions, these habits will already be second nature.

You'll have the confidence and knowledge to make choices that help you achieve your goals and enjoy life. So, the next time you receive $20, think about what that money could do for you beyond today. Whether you save it or invest it, each choice brings you closer to a future where you're in control, and your money is working as hard as you do.

Earning Money

Want to buy that awesome new game or the latest sneakers? Well, your goanna needs some cash! But where does the money come from?

Most grown-ups earn money by working. They have jobs where they get paid for doing something helpful or creating something cool. For example:

- **Teachers** educate students and help them learn new things.
- **Doctors** treat people and keep them healthy.
- **Chefs** prepare delicious meals for others to enjoy.

- **Delivery drivers** make sure packages and food get to your doorstep

The payment they get from doing this is called a **salary (monthly based)** or **wage (based on contract; hourly or daily)**.

If you've ever thought about what kind of job you want when you grow up, you'll know there are many options! Some jobs require lots of schooling, like being a doctor or a scientist, while others might need special training, like becoming a pilot or a chef. Do you also know that the amount of money you can earn depends on the type of job you have. Some jobs pay more than others, but what really matters is to find a job you enjoy so you do not get frustrated in the long run!

Let's focus on now!

You do not have to wait until you have a college degree before you start making money. As a kid, you can also make money and there are many cool ways to start earning, too.

Here are some ideas:

- Taking care of pets or Walking dogs
- Organizing rooms or closets
- Washing cars
- Watering plants for neighbors on vacation
- Setting up a refreshment stand
- Helping with garden work
- Collecting recyclables

You can also use your skills to make money.

- Teaching younger kids, a sport you're good at
- Making and selling crafts
- Helping older neighbors with technology
- Tutoring in your best subjects
- Creating birthday cards or holiday decorations

But working for someone else isn't the only way to earn money. You can also start your own business! Think about it: maybe you're amazing at baking cookies or building robots. You could sell your creations and make a profit! Profit is the money you make after you pay for all the things you need for your business, like ingredients or supplies. For example, if you sell a robot for $20 and it costs you $5 to build it, your profit is $15!

Running a business can be challenging, but it's also super rewarding. You get to be your own boss and make your own decisions. Plus, it's a great way to learn about money and how to manage it. When you spend money, you've earned yourself, you tend to think twice about how to use it because you know exactly how much effort it took to make it!

So, whether you dream of being a firefighter, a video game designer, or the owner of the coolest toy store in town, remember that earning money takes hard work and dedication. Always talk to your parents first about any money-earning ideas to make sure they're safe and okay with them. But with a little effort and creativity, you can achieve your goals and get that money!

Smart Spending

Spending money can feel exciting, especially when you have a little extra cash in your pocket. Whether going out for ice cream with friends, buying a new game, or getting something you've been wanting for weeks, spending time can be fun. But not all spending is equal.

Why?

Because there are needs and there are wants. Needs are things you can't go without, like food, basic clothing, and school supplies. They're essential items that help you live well and stay healthy. Wants, on the other hand, are things that are nice to have but aren't necessary, like new video games, movie tickets, or trendy sneakers.

Understanding the difference between needs and wants is the first step to spending smartly. It helps you make choices that fit your goals rather than just going for what seems fun at the moment. For example, if you've been saving for a new game but see a cool pair of shoes that everyone's wearing, you might feel tempted to spend your money right away on that. But when you know what you're saving for and what matters most to you, it's easier to pause and decide if that purchase is truly worth it.

Once you're clear on your needs and wants, here are some tips for making smart choices when it's time to spend:

Think Before You Buy

When you see something, you want, pause and ask yourself a few questions: Do I really need this? Will I still want it in a week or a month? Could I find a better price somewhere else? Taking a moment to think before spending can help you avoid buying things you don't actually want as much as you thought.

Set a Spending Limit

It's easy to get carried away when you're out shopping, especially if you have money saved up. Setting a spending limit for yourself—like deciding to spend only $5 or $10—helps you stay in control. This way, you can enjoy buying something you want without draining your savings.

Look for Deals and Discounts

One of the smartest ways to spend is by finding deals and discounts. If there's something you've been wanting, wait for a sale or check if there's a discount available. You can also go the extra mile of checking different stores to see which sells at a cheaper rate. This way, you get what you want while having extra cash after.

Avoid Impulse Buys

Impulse buys are those "sudden" purchases you make without thinking, like grabbing candy at the checkout counter or picking up a toy just because it looks cool at the moment. While it's okay to do this sometimes, too many impulse buys can quickly eat up your savings. One helpful strategy is to wait before buying. If you see something you want but didn't plan for, pause and give yourself at least a day to think it over.

Ask Yourself: Is It Worth It?

Before buying something, think about the value it will bring you. Will it last a long time? Will you still enjoy it in a month or year? Sometimes spending a bit more on something of higher quality or that will last longer is smarter than buying something cheap that breaks easily or isn't as fun as you thought.

One important lesson is that smart spending doesn't mean you can't enjoy your money. In fact, it's about finding a balance that lets you enjoy spending while still keeping your goals in mind. For example, you might set aside some of your money each month specifically for fun things like snacks or games, while the rest goes toward savings or a bigger goal. This way, you get to enjoy your money now without putting your future goals at risk.

Creating a simple budget can help you practice smart spending. Imagine a budget like a game plan for your money. It's a way to keep track of how much money you receive and how you spend it. Just like a sports team plans their strategy, a budget helps you plan your financial moves. Whether you're getting an allowance, birthday money, or earnings from small jobs, a budget helps you understand where your money goes and how to make the most of it.

To make a budget, you must first write down all your income and expenses. Income is the money you receive. For you, this might include:

- Allowance from parents
- Money from part-time jobs
- Gift money
- Earnings from chores or small side gigs

Expenses are the money you spend. This could be:

- Snacks and drinks
- Phone credit
- Entertainment (movies, games)
- Saving for something special
- Gifts for friends and family

Once you've listed your income and expenses, the next step is to compare them. This is where the magic of budgeting happens! Look at how much money you're bringing in and how much you're spending. Are your expenses higher than your income? If so, you'll need to make some choices.

Divide your money into three parts:

Spend – Use this for things you want, like snacks or small treats.

Save – Set aside some for later, especially for future goals or big purchases.

Stash – Keep a small amount for any unexpected expenses or emergency buys

Use the 50/30/20 principle to allocate funds to these three categories:

- 50% for necessary expenses
- 30% for things you want/unexpected buys
- 20% for savings

Once you've divided your money using the 50/30/20 rule, this is where budgeting really starts to come in handy. Let's take a closer look at each category to see how you can plan and allocate your funds effectively. We'll start with Spend, which covers your necessary expenses.

Step 1: Break Down Your Spending Needs

In the **Spend** category (50% of your income), list everything you absolutely need to spend money on. For example:

- School lunches
- Transportation (bus fare, gas, etc.)
- Basic supplies (notebooks, pens, or other school items)
- Personal care items (toothpaste, soap, etc.)

Now, allocate part of your 50% budget to each item. Let's assume your monthly income is $100. Your Spend category gives you $50 to work with. Here's how you could allocate it:

- **School Lunches:** $20
- **Transportation:** $15

- **Basic Supplies:** $10
- **Personal Care:** $5

Total: $50

Step 2: Does Your Budget Cover Everything?

Now, compare your list of necessary expenses to the 50% allocated for spending:

- Does your $50 cover everything on your list?
- If not, you'll need to **prioritize** or **improvise**.

For instance:

- If transportation costs are higher than $15, can you pack lunch from home to reduce lunch costs?
- If you need more for supplies, can you cut back on personal care items this month and restock them later?

Step 3: Plan for the Other Categories

Once you've worked out your **Spend** category, move on to **Stash** (30%) and **Save** (20%).

For Stash (30%): This part of your budget covers wants and unexpected expenses. Let's say you have $30 allocated here.

Examples:

- Buy a $10 snack or treat with friends.
- Spend $5 on a new app or small hobby item.
- Leave $15 for emergency buys, like replacing a broken charger.

For Save (20%): This is for your future goals or emergency funds. With $20 allocated here, you could divide it further:

- $5 goes into your savings for a big purchase, like a game or bike.
- $5 stays in a savings emergency fund.

- $10 stays in an investment savings fund.

Step 4: Adjust and Improve

If your spending doesn't fit neatly into the 50/30/20 plan, it's a signal to adjust your priorities. For example:

- Are there ways to save on transportation, like carpooling or walking?
- Can you lower your "wants" spending in Stash to free up more for necessities or savings?

The most important part of budgeting is tracking. This means writing down every time you receive or spend money. You can use:

- A notebook
- Budgeting apps like Greenlight, FamZoo, Busy Kid, Rooster Money.
- Spreadsheets
- Notes on your phone

Budgeting is all about making these small decisions to ensure your money works for you. Practice this every time you get money, and it'll soon become second nature!

Simple Budgeting Worksheet

Category	Planned Amount ($)	Actual Amount ($)
Total Income		
Necessary Expenses (50%)		
1.		
2.		
3.		
4.		
Wants/Unexpected Buys (30%)		

1.		
2.		
3.		
Savings (20%)		
1.		
2.		

The Teen Budget Worksheet from FamilyEducation is a helpful budget template to work with.

The Power of Giving Back

When we think about money, we often focus on how to spend it or save it for ourselves. But there's another powerful way to use money: donating. Donating means giving a part of your money, time, or resources to help others, whether it is supporting a charity, contributing to a cause you care about, or helping someone in need.

Why is donating important?

It helps make the world a better place. When you donate, you're contributing to something bigger than yourself. You could help provide food for families, school supplies for kids, or even protect endangered animals. It's also a way to show kindness, gratitude, and responsibility as a community member. Plus, it feels great to know you've positively impacted someone's life.

If you want to start donating, the good news is you don't need a lot of money to make a difference. Here's how to plan for it:

Decide How Much to Donate

Set aside a small portion of your income, like 5-10%. For example, if you get $100 a month, you could donate $5 to a cause you care about.

Choose a Cause You Believe In

Think about what matters most to you. Here are some ideas:

- Supporting a local animal shelter

- Helping kids access school supplies
- Contributing to disaster relief efforts
- Donating to medical research for diseases like cancer or diabetes
- Supporting environmental projects like planting trees or cleaning up beaches

Find Reputable Charities.

You can also look for smaller, local charities in your community to donate to.

Incorporating Donations into Your 50/30/20 Budget

Here's how donations can fit into your budgeting plan:

- **Spend (50%)**: If your donation involves buying items for a cause, like canned goods for a food drive, include it here.
- **Stash (30%)**: Set aside part of your "wants" or "unexpected buys" budget for donations. For instance, you could skip a snack one week and use that money to donate.

- **Save (20%)**: Create a small "charity fund" in your savings. Over time, this money can grow and be used for larger donations.

If you don't have cash to donate, you can still give back by:

- Donating your time by volunteering.
- Giving away items you no longer use, like clothes, toys, or books.
- Organizing a fundraising event, like a bake sale or charity run.

Donating isn't about how much you give; it's about the thought and effort you put into helping others. Even a small act of kindness can create a ripple effect of positivity. So next time you plan your budget, consider setting aside a little for someone who needs it.

Online and ATM Safety

Handling money comes with a responsibility to keep it safe. You know once you open a bank account and start keeping money there, that version of your money is digital? With your digital money. You can easily use a card to make purchases or easily pay with your phone. You're basically using real money that's stored in your bank account - it's just easier than carrying lots of cash around.

Now, when we talk about "money safety," we mean protecting both your actual cash and the bank information connected to it, like your passwords, bank account details, and personal identification numbers (PINs). This information is sensitive because it's directly linked to your money, and if someone else gains access to it, they could use it without your permission.

So, where does this information come from, and why does it matter?

At some point, you might open a bank account with the help of your parents or a guardian. When you open a bank account, you'll receive details like an account number and a PIN (Personal Identification Number). This is where safety measures start to become important. These details give you access to your account, allowing you to check your balance, keep (deposit) money, or make purchases. Since these numbers are unique to your account, it's essential to keep them private. Think of it as your personal key to your money box—you wouldn't give that to a stranger right? In the same way, you shouldn't share your bank details with others.

Along with your bank account, you might also receive a debit card. A debit card looks like a credit card, but it works a bit differently. When you use a debit card, you're spending the money you already have in your account, rather than borrowing money. Your debit card can be used for purchases online or in stores, as well as to withdraw cash from an ATM.

To use your debit card, you need a PIN. Your PIN is a four-digit code that acts like a password for your debit card. When you enter your PIN at an ATM or during a purchase, you're confirming that you're the owner of the account and have permission to use the funds. Protecting your PIN is very important—if someone else knows it, they could potentially use your card to take money from your account. Keeping your PIN private and memorizing it instead of writing it down, is one of the first safety habits to develop. Now, while ATMs are super convenient, there's a lot more to using them safely than just covering the keypad when you type your PIN.

Your debit card has some very important information on it—information that needs to stay private. This includes the long card number on the front, the expiry date, and a special three-digit code on the back called the CVV (Card Verification Value). These details are just as important as your PIN, and here's why: even if someone doesn't have your card, they can use these numbers to make online purchases without your permission. That's why it's crucial to understand how to keep these details safe.

First, let's talk about the card number. That's the long number on the front of your debit card, and it's unique to your account. When you buy something online, you're usually asked to enter this number. It's like your card's digital fingerprint, and it should be kept as private as your phone password. Then, there's the expiry date, which tells you when the card stops working. Scammers need this date along with the card number to make purchases online. Finally, on the back of your card, you'll find the CVV—a three-digit number that's used as an extra layer of security for online shopping.

Now that you know what these numbers are, let's talk about keeping them safe. First rule: never share your card information with anyone. If someone asks for your card number, expiry date, or CVV—especially online—the probability of it being a scam is very high. Even if they say it's for a contest, a prize, or a free offer, don't fall for it. Real companies will never ask you to share this information in messages or posts.

Another big No-No: don't post pictures of your debit/credit card. Sometimes, scammers trick people into taking a photo of their card by pretending that there is a reward or a giveaway. No matter how exciting the offer sounds, keep your card out of photos. Once someone has your card number, expiry date, and CVV, they can use them to shop online like it's their own card.

Finally, keep an eye on your bank account. Make it a habit to check your account regularly (with your parents if you need help) to see if all the transactions look right. If you notice something you didn't do, let your parents and bank know immediately. The faster you catch a mistake, the easier it is to fix.

Staying Safe with Online Transfers

With a bank account, you have the privilege to make online transactions. If you've ever bought something online or sent money using a phone app, you're probably already familiar with online transfers. While they're convenient, they come with some risks if you're not careful. So, there are a few tips you should follow.

First, when making purchases or transfers online, always use websites or apps that are trusted and secure. Remember in earlier chapters where I taught you how to check for how a site is secured? You look for a small padlock icon or "https" in the website address—these are signs that the site is safe. If you're not sure about a site, ask a parent or adult to help you check if it's trustworthy.

Second, your account information, passwords, and PINs are private and should never be shared. Even close friends shouldn't know this information. Just like you wouldn't give someone the key to your locker in school, you shouldn't share details that could let others access your money.

Third, before you complete any online transfer, take a moment to double-check the details. Is the amount correct? Are you sending it to the right person or place? A simple mistake in the account number could cause a problem, so make it a habit to check twice before hitting "send."

Withdrawing Cash Safely

ATMs (Automated Teller Machines) make it easy to withdraw cash, but there are a few simple steps you should follow to ensure your safety when using one.

Choose Safe Locations

If you need to use an ATM, pick one in a safe, well-lit place, preferably inside a bank. Avoid ATMs in isolated areas, especially at night. When ATMs are in busy, visible locations, you're less likely to run into problems.

Be Aware of Your Surroundings

Before you start using the ATM, take a quick look around to ensure it feels safe. Trust your instincts—if anything feels off, come back later or find another ATM. Being aware of what's happening around you helps you stay alert and safe while accessing your money.

Protect Your PIN

When you enter your PIN at the ATM, cover the keypad with your hand to keep it private. This small habit prevents others from seeing your PIN. Also, avoid using easy-to-guess numbers like your birthdate—choose something memorable to you but hard for others to figure out.

PRACTICAL EXERCISE 8

1. Write down one thing you've been wanting to buy. Is it a need or a want? Why?

____

____

____

____

____

2. Look at your weekly allowance or earnings. Divide it into **Save**, **Spend**, and **Stash** categories. Write down your plan:

- Save: $________
- Spend: $________
- Stash: $________

3. Write down three things you've spent money on in the past month. Next to each, write whether it was a good

choice or something you regret. What would you do differently next time?

____

____

____

____

____

4. Start tracking your money this week. Write down all the money you receive and spend. At the end of the week, answer these questions:

- How much did you save?

____

- How much did you spend?

____

- What surprised you about how you used your money?

____

Weekly Money Management Checklist

Use this checklist every week to make sure you're building good habits:

- € I saved a portion of my money for future goals.
- € I tracked all my spending to see where my money went.
- € I reviewed my savings progress and adjusted if needed.
- € I thought carefully about every purchase before spending.
- € I avoided sharing my PIN, card number, or other sensitive details.
- € I practiced keeping my money safe while using ATMs or online apps.
- € I talked to my parents or guardians about improving my money habits.
- € I checked my account or savings balance to make sure it matched my records.

“If you want to live a happy life, tie it to a goal not people or things”

- *Albert Einstein*

SKILL 9: SET GOALS WITH PURPOSE

Welcome to the final habit in this journey of developing essential life skills. Each habit we've discussed plays a unique role in building confidence, making smart decisions, and helping you grow into a capable and responsible person. In this last chapter, we'll focus on setting and achieving goals purposefully. If the habits in this book are tools, then setting goals is like having a compass

Setting and Achieving Goals

A goal is simply something you want to achieve. It could be anything from mastering a new video game to getting a good grade on a test. But setting goals isn't just about saying, "I want to do this." It's about deciding who you want to be, what you want to achieve, and how you'll get there. Goals turn dreams into plans and plans into actions. Without goals, even the most talented people can waste time and energy on things that don't matter. But with clear goals, you know exactly where to focus your efforts and how to measure your progress.

Think of a goal as a destination. If you don't know where you're going, any road will take you there—and you might end up somewhere you don't want to be. But if you have a clear destination in mind, you can choose the best path to get there, step by step. For example, if your goal is to learn how to ride a bike, you might start by practicing balance. Once you've mastered that, you can focus on pedaling and steering until you're confident enough to ride on your own.

Goals give you purpose. When you set a goal, you decide what's important to you. This focus helps you make better decisions because you know what you're working toward. Let's say your goal is to save $100 to buy a new bike. You're less likely to spend your allowance on snacks or games because you know it'll slow you down from reaching your goal.

Goals also help you grow. Every time you set a goal; you challenge yourself to do something you haven't done before. This might mean learning a new skill, improving a habit, or stepping out of your comfort zone. The process of working toward a goal teaches you discipline, patience, and resilience—all traits that help you succeed in other areas of life.

Many people get stuck because their goals feel too big. They think, "How can I ever do that?" But the secret to achieving big goals is breaking them into smaller steps. Each small step brings you closer to the finish line, and before you know it, you've accomplished something amazing.

Let's say your goal is to run a 5-mile race. That might sound intimidating if you've never run more than a few blocks. But instead of focusing on the full 5 miles, you could start with smaller steps, like running for 5 minutes without stopping, then 10 minutes, and so on. Every small win builds your confidence and momentum.

Breaking goals into smaller steps also makes them more manageable. When a goal is too big, it's easy to procrastinate or feel discouraged. But when you focus on one small step at a time, you'll feel motivated to keep going.

Jake was 13 years old and loved soccer. Every day after school, he practiced with his friends, dreaming of playing on his school's soccer team. But Jake faced a big challenge: he wasn't the strongest player. Many of the kids trying out had been playing on teams for years, while Jake had only played casually. It would have been easy for him to give up, but Jake decided to set a goal.

Jake's goal was simple but meaningful: to improve his soccer skills and make the team at tryouts. He knew this wouldn't happen overnight, so he broke his goal into smaller steps. He made a schedule to practice dribbling, passing, and shooting for 30 minutes every day. He also asked his dad for help creating a workout routine to build his strength and stamina.

At first, progress was slow. Jake missed shots and fumbled passes. But he kept going. Every day, Jake got a little better. After a few weeks, Jake noticed he could control the ball more easily and run faster without getting tired. His friends started noticing, too, and joined him for extra practice. By the time tryouts came, Jake was ready. Not only did he make the team, but his coach praised him for his hard work and improvement.

Jake's story shows that achieving a goal isn't about being perfect from the start. It's about setting a target, making a plan, and sticking with it—even when it's hard. Along the way, Jake learned discipline, built confidence, and proved to himself that he could succeed if he put in the effort.

One of the best tools for setting meaningful goals is the SMART method. You may remember this from Chapter 1: SMART goals are **Specific, Measurable, Achievable, Relevant,** and **Time-bound.**

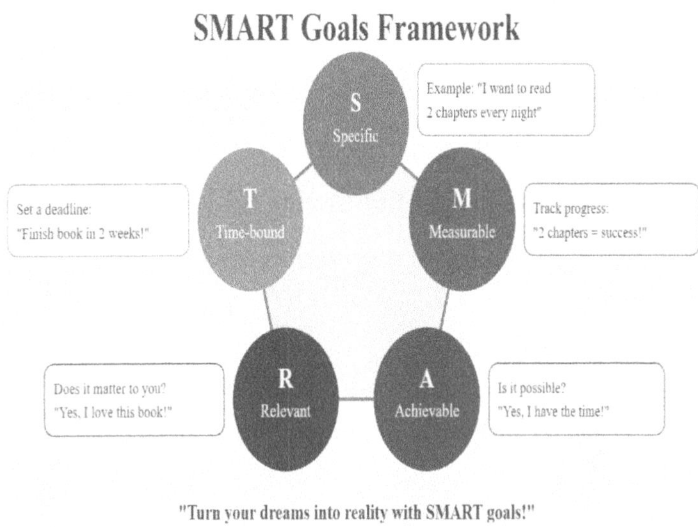

Let's break each of these down again with examples to show how they work in real life.

Specific

A specific goal is clear and focused. Instead of saying, "I want to get better at basketball," a specific goal would be, "I want to improve my free-throw accuracy to 80%." When you make your goal specific, it's easier to know exactly what you're working toward.

Measurable

A measurable goal means you can track your progress. For example, if your goal is to save money, you might set a measurable target, like saving $5 each week. Seeing your progress gives you motivation to keep going.

Achievable

Goals should be challenging but realistic. If you've never run before, setting a goal to run a marathon next month isn't achievable. Instead, aim to run one mile without stopping and gradually increase the distance.

Relevant

Your goal should be something that matters to you. If you set a goal just because someone else thinks you should, you're less likely to stay motivated. Choose goals that are connected to your interests and values.

Time-bound

A time-bound goal has a deadline. Without a time limit, it's easy to procrastinate. For example, instead of saying, "I'll learn to play guitar someday," say, "I'll learn to play three chords by the end of this month."

Let's see how Jake's goal to make the soccer team could fit into the SMART framework:

- **Specific**: Jake wanted to improve his soccer skills and make the team.
- **Measurable**: He tracked his progress by practicing specific drills every day.
- **Achievable**: Jake didn't aim to be the best player overnight; he focused on steady improvement, progress over perfection.
- **Relevant**: Making the team was important to Jake because he loved soccer.

- **Time-bound**: He set a clear deadline: the date of the team tryouts.

Using the SMART method, Jake turned his dream into a plan, and that plan helped him succeed.

Practical Tips for Goal-Setting Success

Now that you understand how to set goals, here are some practical tips to help you stay on track:

Write It Down

Your brain is powerful, but it can get busy with thousands of thoughts each day. Writing down your goals is like dropping an anchor – it keeps your dreams from drifting away. A goal journal doesn't have to be fancy. Even a simple notebook works great. Write down what you want to achieve, when you want to achieve it, and the steps you'll take to get there. You might write: "By June 1st, I want to learn three new skateboard tricks. I'll practice for 30 minutes after school on Tuesdays and Thursdays." Each time you look at your written goals, you're reminding yourself of what matters to you.

Start Small

Think of building a LEGO set. You don't throw all the pieces together at once – you start with a simple foundation and add pieces one by one. Goals work the same way. Want to learn coding? Start with 15 minutes of practice each day. Want to save money? Begin with putting aside just one dollar a day or a month. These small steps might not seem like much, but they add up fast. Plus, starting small helps you build confidence and momentum. Before you know it, those small steps become powerful habits.

Tell Someone

Sharing your goals is like having a spotter when you're lifting weights – they're there to support you and help you succeed. When you tell a friend, parent, or teacher about your goals, you're creating your own support team. They can cheer you on when things get tough, give advice when you're stuck, and celebrate with you when you succeed. Plus, knowing that someone else knows about your goal can give you that extra push to keep going when you feel like giving up.

Create Reminders

Your phone buzzes to remind you about homework. Your alarm clock wakes you up for school. So why not create reminders for your goals too? Put sticky notes on your bathroom mirror. Set a daily phone alarm. Make your goal your phone's wallpaper. These constant reminders are like friendly nudges throughout your day, keeping your goals front and center in your mind. For example, if your goal is to drink more water, put a water bottle sticker on your school folder. Every time you see it, you'll think, "Oh yeah, time for some water!"

Be Patient

Success rarely happens overnight. Think about your favorite video game – you don't beat the final boss on your first try. You level up slowly, gaining skills and experience along the way. Goals work the same way. Some days you'll feel like you're crushing it, and other days might feel like you're stuck. That's totally normal. The key is to keep showing up, even on the tough days. Remember: slow progress is still progress.

Tracking Your Progress and Tools to Help

Writing down your progress is super important when you're trying to reach your goals. If you don't keep track, you might forget how much you've improved or miss some of the small wins along the way. There are many cool ways to track your goals. If you like writing, a simple notebook works great. You can make a list of small goals and check them off when you finish them.

If you're into technology, you can use your phone to track goals. Apps like Google Keep, Strides, Todoist, Toodledo, or even your phone's notes app work well. These apps can remind you about your goals and help you update how you're doing. For instance, if you want to save up for something, you can use an app to track your money.

You can also make tracking fun. For instance, if you're saving money, you can draw a big thermometer and color it in as your savings grow. Or if you're learning something new, like playing basketball, color in your calendar every day you practice.

The most important thing is to update your tracking every day or every week. This helps you stay focused and lets you fix any problems quickly. Even when it feels like you're moving slowly, looking at your tracker will show you how far you've come!

Learn From Setbacks

Have you ever watched a skateboarder trying to nail a new trick? They fall - a lot. But each fall teaches them something new about what works and what doesn't. Setbacks in your goals are just like those falls – they're not failures, they're feedback. Maybe you missed a few days of practicing your instrument, or you spent your savings on something you didn't need. Don't beat yourself up. Instead, ask yourself: "What can I learn from this? How can I do better next time?" Then get back up and try again.

Celebrate Wins

Reaching a goal feels awesome, but don't wait until the end to celebrate. Celebrating small wins along the way is like giving yourself a high-five – it keeps you pumped and motivated. Did you stick to your study schedule all week? Awesome! Reward yourself with some extra game time. Did you save your first $50? Maybe treat yourself to something small while keeping most of your savings. These celebrations remind you that working toward your goals can be fun, not just hard work.

Remember, these tips aren't rules set in stone. Try them out and see which ones work best for you. Mix and match them, adapt them, make them your own. The most important thing is finding what keeps you moving forward toward your goals.

PRACTICAL EXERCISE 9

1. What is your goal? Write it down clearly. Be as specific as possible.

____

____

____

____

____

2. Think about how achieving this goal will make you feel and what difference it will make in your life.

____

____

____

____

3. What are the first three small steps you can take to get started?

Step 1:

____

____

____

Step 2:

____

____

____

Step 3:

____

____

____

4. Write out what comes next and how you'll keep building on your progress.

____

____

5. What is your deadline for each small step?

Step 1 Deadline:

Step 2 Deadline:

Step 3 Deadline:

6. How will you track your progress? Write down the method you'll use (e.g., notebook, app, or calendar).

7. How often will you review your progress? Decide if you'll check in daily, weekly, or monthly.

____

____

8. What will you do if you face challenges or fall behind? Plan how you'll adjust your steps or timeline if needed.

____

____

____

____

9. What small rewards can you give yourself along the way? Example: Treat yourself to something fun after completing a big step.

____

Now, to commit to your plan, write this as a promise to yourself:

> **"I commit to working toward my goal, step by step, and I will not give up, even if it gets hard. I believe in my ability to succeed and will do my best to make this happen."**

CONCLUSION

Congratulations, you've made it! You've conquered nine essential skills – a feat more impressive than scaling Mount Everest (probably). As we turn to the last page of '9 Essential Skills to Master – Boys 8-14', I invite you to reflect not just on the skills themselves but on the transformative journey they represent. Each chapter has been carefully crafted to inspire growth, instill confidence, and unlock potential in you at a pivotal stage of your life. These are not just lessons for the moment; they are lifelong principles that will guide your actions, choices, and relationships. This book is a toolkit for your transformation, a beacon that illuminates the path from potential to greatness. Each skill is a step toward a life of purpose and fulfillment, a foundation for navigating the complexities of the modern world with grace and determination.

Over the course of this guide, you've learned about nine powerful skills that can help you grow, succeed, and handle life's challenges. These skills aren't just tasks to finish—they're tools you can use every day to get better, stay strong, and achieve your goals. Let's take a moment to go over what we've covered and the key lessons from each chapter.

We started with **'Optimistic Adaptability' - The Power Trio - Practicing Gratitude, Positivity and Accepting Change**. This is a habit that helps you focus on the good things in your life instead of what you don't have. Gratitude is more than just saying "thank you"—it's about noticing and appreciating the small and big positives around you. By being grateful every day, you create a mindset that stays strong even when life gets hard. Being Positive gives you a fresh perspective on events and how to react to situations as they arise in our lives and Change helps us to adapt to new situations and environments with an open mind, focusing on what we can control to move along in the right direction with the right frame of mind.

Next came **Basic Domestic Skills**, like cooking, cleaning, and taking care of your personal hygiene. These simple but important skills are the foundation of independence. When you know how to keep your space clean, prepare a healthy meal, and dress well, you're taking steps to take care of yourself and feel confident.

In **Developing Your Personality**, we talked about responsibility, accountability, and problem-solving. Taking responsibility means owning up to your actions and their outcomes, good or bad. Problem-solving and critical thinking help you handle challenges with a calm and clear mind. These habits build your character and make you a dependable person who can overcome difficulties.

Then, we explored **Learning Effective Communication**, which is all about expressing yourself clearly and listening to others with respect. Good communication helps you build strong friendships, solve problems peacefully, and ensure your ideas are heard.

Teamwork and Collaboration reminded us that we're stronger together. Whether it's a group project or a team sport, learning how to work well with others teaches you how to share ideas, support each other, and achieve goals as a team.

With **Empathy and Emotional Intelligence**, we learned how to understand feelings—both our own and others'. When you recognize emotions, you can connect better with people, solve conflicts calmly, and strengthen your relationships. Along with empathy, we talked about **Resilience**, or bouncing back from setbacks. Whether it's a tough test or a difficult day, resilience helps you stay strong and keep moving forward.

In today's world, **Digital Literacy** is a must-have skill. Knowing how to balance screen time, avoid online scams, and protect your personal information helps you use technology wisely. Being smart about how you use the internet sets you apart and keeps you safe.

We also talked about **Financial Literacy**, where we learnt about money, why it is important, the different types of money, and credit and debit cards. We also explored avenues on how to manage money, save wisely, and even invest. Learning how to track spending, create a budget, and keep your money safe online are all important steps toward becoming financially independent.

Finally, in **Setting Goals with Purpose**, we learned about goals and how to use them to turn dreams into action. Setting clear, meaningful goals that are specific, measurable, achievable, relevant, and timebound by breaking them into small, achievable steps helps you focus on what matters and celebrate your progress along the way.

Nine Habits for Success

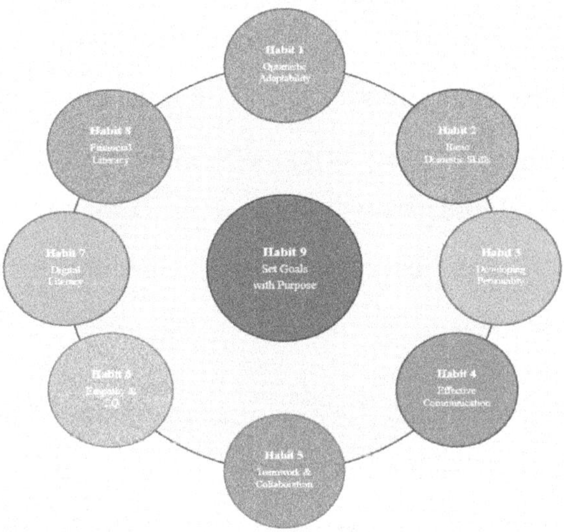

Each of these skills connects to the others, creating a toolkit you can use for the rest of your life. Together, they make you stronger, more capable, more confident, and better prepared to handle whatever life throws your way.

This is not the end of your journey—it's a beginning. With these tools, you are equipped to forge your own path, build meaningful connections, and tackle challenges with courage and creativity. My hope is that this book serves as both a guide and a spark, igniting a passion for lifelong learning and personal growth within you. As you close this book, remember: the skills mastered here are seeds sown in fertile soil. Nurtured with love, guidance, and encouragement, they will grow into a legacy of strength, kindness, and integrity. Life is a journey of learning and growing. Every day brings new chances to practice these skills and find new ways to improve. You don't need to get everything perfect right now—change happens one step at a time.

Here's a challenge for you: pick one habit from this book to focus on each week. Write down how you'll practice it, and check in at the end of the week to see how you did. Maybe you'll write three things you're grateful for each night or work on listening more to your friends and family. Whatever habit you choose, stick to it and see how it changes your life.

Remember, success isn't about being perfect—it's about trying your best, learning from mistakes, and keeping at it. You have everything you need to be your best self. These habits are your starting point. Use them, build on them, and never stop growing.

"Success is the sum of small efforts, repeated day in and day out." – *Robert Collier*

Take what you've learned and show the world what you're capable of. Start small, stay determined, and keep growing. Your future self will thank you for starting today. For real though, you've equipped yourselves with tools that will serve you well throughout life. Now it's your turn go forth and use them! Tackle those challenges, build amazing friendships, and learn to juggle flaming chainsaws (kidding... mostly). But seriously, the world is waiting. Go make it awesome.

You've got this!

WHAT DID YOU THINK?

Nothing is more annoying than someone asking for a review, but unfortunately, they 'matter'. As a budding writer who wants to give his best to his readers - it matters a lot. Therefore, if you liked my effort during this read, I would be extremely grateful if you would take a moment to leave behind a quick five-star review. Honestly, it can be super short (or super long, if that's you), but even a star rating without any words can do wonders for me. If you were bothered by something, whether a typo, grammatical mistake or anything else, I'd love to hear about it and will do my best to fix it right away! Without all of you, I would not be able to do this, and I would have to struggle at my age to get a real job again **SHUDDER**. Therefore, if you would be willing to leave a review, that would be incredible. But even if you don't, I just want you to know that I am extremely grateful that you gave my work a chance and made it this far. Seriously, you are the best!

A big thank you from my heart.

RESOURCES

Apps

- Canva: https://www.canva.com/
- CapCut: https://www.capcut.com/
- Google Slides: https://workspace.google.com/products/slides/
- Greenlight: https://greenlight.com/
- iMovie: https://www.apple.com/imovie/
- RoosterMoney: https://roostermoney.com/
- Scratch: https://scratch.mit.edu/
- TikTok: https://www.tiktok.com/
- YouTube: https://www.youtube.com/

Sites

- Doctors Without Borders: https://www.doctorswithoutborders.org/
- Feeding America: https://www.feedingamerica.org/
- StopCyberBullying.org: https://www.stopcyberbullying.org/
- Stay Safe Online: https://staysafeonline.org/

- StopNCII.org: https://stopncii.org/
- UNICEF: https://www.unicef.org/lac/en/digital-skills-development
- World Wildlife Fund: https://www.worldwildlife.org/

REFERENCES

- Daniel Wong. (2024, April 8). *Communication skills for teens*. Retrieved from https://www.daniel-wong.com/2024/04/08/communication-skills-for-teens/
- Daily Mail. (2015, March 23). *The science of folding clothes: Robotics engineers reveal the technique for packing garments into neat squares*. Retrieved from https://www.dailymail.co.uk/sciencetech/article-3004164/The-science-FOLDING-CLOTHES-Robotics-engineers-reveal-technique-packing-garments-neat-squares.html
- FamilyEducation. (n.d.). *Teen budget worksheet.* Retrieved from https://www.familyeducation.com/teens/values-responsibilities/jobs-money/teen-budget-worksheet
- Gimme Some Oven. (n.d.). *Everyday salad recipe*. Retrieved from

https://www.gimmesomeoven.com/everyday-salad-recipe/#tasty-recipes-60359

- Heart-Mind Online. (n.d.). *Teens connecting with others: Reflective communication*. Retrieved from https://heartmindonline.org/resources/teens-connecting-with-others-reflective-communication
- Healthline. (n.d.). *Vinegar in laundry*. Retrieved from https://www.healthline.com/health/vinegar-in-laundry#:~:text=Vinegar%20doesn't%20usually%20stain,pouring%20it%20onto%20your%20clothing
- iStock. (n.d.). *Infographics with man showing proper and improper body postures for standing*. Retrieved from https://www.istockphoto.com/vector/infographics-with-man-showing-proper-and-improper-body-postures-for-standing-gm1843635857-551511079
- Invite Japan. (n.d.). *Team-building games*. Retrieved from https://www.invitejapan.com/en/team-building-games/#:~:text=Two%20Truths%20and%20a%20

Lie.%20%E2%80%9CTwo%20Truths,true%2C%20and%20one%20that%20is%20a%20lie

- Investopedia. (n.d.). *The three S's of simple investing*. Retrieved from https://www.investopedia.com/articles/basics/11/3-s-simple-investing.asp
- JoyFoodSunshine. (n.d.). *How to make an omelette*. Retrieved from https://joyfoodsunshine.com/omelette-recipe/
- KidsHealth. (n.d.). *Cuts and grazes: First aid.* Retrieved from https://kidshealth.org/en/parents/cuts-sheet.html
- Kids Financial Education. (n.d.). *Advice for ages 14–16*. Retrieved from https://www.kidsfinancialeducation.com/advice/ages-14-16/
- Love and Lemons. (n.d.). *Scrambled eggs recipe.* Retrieved from https://www.loveandlemons.com/scrambled-eggs-recipe/#wprm-recipe-container-57863
- May Clinic. (n.d.). *First aid for burns*. Retrieved from https://www.mayoclinic.org/first-aid/first-aid-burns/basics/art-

20056649#:~:text=Hold%20the%20area%20under%20cool,rings%20or%20other%20tight%20items

- May Clinic. (n.d.). *First aid for cuts*. Retrieved from https://www.mayoclinic.org/first-aid/first-aid-cuts/basics/art-20056711
- MDPI. (2023). *The social structures of relationships*. *Societies, 13*(6), 148. Retrieved from https://www.mdpi.com/2075-4698/13/6/148
- MotivateUs. (n.d.). *The blind boy*. Retrieved from https://motivateus.com/stories/the-blind-boy.htm
- NHS. (n.d.). *Cuts and grazes: First aid*. Retrieved from https://www.nhs.uk/conditions/cuts-and-grazes/#:~:text=Clean%20the%20wound%20by%20rinsing,sterile%20dressing%20or%20a%20plaster
- Positive Psychology. (n.d.). *Mentally strong*. Retrieved from https://positivepsychology.com/mentally-strong/
- Stanford Children's Health. (n.d.). *Relationship development for teens*. Retrieved from https://www.stanfordchildrens.org/en/topic/default?id=relationship-development-90-P01642

- Speed Queen. (n.d.). *Secrets to stopping colors from bleeding and fading*. Retrieved from https://speedqueen.com/scoop-blog/laundry-room/tips/the-secrets-to-stopping-colors-from-bleeding-and-fading/#:~:text=Add%201%20cup%20of%20vinegar,black%20jeans%20time%20and%20again
- Teen Coach Academy. (n.d.). *Developing emotional resilience in teens*. Retrieved from https://teencoachacademy.com/blog/developing-emotional-resilience-in-teens/
- TSCFM. (n.d.). *Hacks for students to remember what they study*. Retrieved from https://tscfm.org/news/hacks-for-students-to-remember-what-they-study/
- UNICEF. (n.d.). *Digital skills development for youth*. Retrieved from https://www.unicef.org/lac/en/digital-skills-development
- University of California Office of the President. (n.d.). *How to write SMART goals*. Retrieved from https://www.ucop.edu/local-human-

resources/_files/performance-appraisal/How+to+write+SMART+Goals+v2.pdf

- WikiHow. (n.d.). *How to brew loose-leaf tea.* Retrieved from https://www.wikihow.com/Brew-Loose-Leaf-Tea
- WikiHow. (n.d.). *How to wash your clothes.* Retrieved from https://www.wikihow.com/Wash-Your-Clothes
- Yorkshire Tea. (n.d.). *How to make a proper brew*. Retrieved from https://www.yorkshiretea.co.uk/our-teas/how-to-make-a-proper-brew

NOTES

www.ingramcontent.com/pod-product-compliance
Ingram Content Group UK Ltd.
Pitfield, Milton Keynes, MK11 3LW, UK
UKHW021402190726
13845UKWH00028B/837

9 789334 177640